Texas Weather

Texas Weather

An Anthology of Poetry, Short Fiction, and Nonfiction

Edited by
Terry Dalrymple
Laurence Musgrove

Introduced by
Clay Reynolds

LITERARY PRESS
LAMAR UNIVERSITY

ISBN: 978-1-942956-36-5
Library of Congress Control Number: 2016958124

Front cover art: Laurence Musgrove
Manufactured in the United States

Lamar University Literary Press
Beaumont, Texas

Acknowledgments

Brown, Nathan. "Back to Some Beginning." *My Salvaged Heart.* Mezcalita Press, 2016.

Davis, William Virgil. "A Winter Day." *descant*, vol. 47, 2008.

DeLotto, Jeffrey. "Birds of the Storm God." *Langdon Review of the Arts in Texas*, vol. 5, 2008-2009.

DeLotto, Jeffrey. "Trinity Flood." *San Pedro River Review Special Issue, In Walt McDonald Country,* Winter 2011.

Ellery, Chris. "Dust Devil." *Quarry*, Mountain Muse Press, 2005.

Guidry, Laura Quinn. "Visitor." *Texas Poetry Calendar 2013,* Dos Gatos Press, 2013.

Hammons, Cheryl. "Tornado Alley." *Rattle,* vol. 39, Spring 2013.

Hawkins, J. Todd. "Waiting Inland for the Hurricane." *Texas Poetry Calendar 2011*, Dos Gatos Press, 2011.

Hoerth, Katherine. "How the Body Heals." *Boundless Anthology*, 2015.

Inge, Charles. "Wildness." *Brazos View*, Ink Brush Press, 2010.

Inge, Charles. "The Wind Relentless." *Brazos View*, Ink Brush Press, 2010.

Milligan, Bryce. "Advent's End." *Southwest Review*, Winter 2014.

Milligan, Bryce. "Gray Descending." *Take to the Highway: Arabesques for Travelers*, West End Press, 2016.

morton, karla k. "A Little Flower." *Constant State of Leaping,* Texas Review Press, 2014.

morton, karla k. "Snow Day." *Constant State of Leaping,* Texas Review Press, 2014.

morton, karla k. "Water." *New and Selected Works,* TCU Press, 2010.

Ruffin, Paul. "Storm." *The Man Who Would Be God*, Southern Methodist, 1993.

Ruffin, Paul. "The Storm Cellar." *Storm Cellar*, chapbook, 1987.

Schneider, Steven P. "Indolence in South Texas." *Alabama Literary Review*, vol. 22, no. 1, 2013.

Seale, Jan. "A Private Miracle." TCU Press, 1992.

Seale, Jan. "Rain Dance." *Latitude* 30° 18', 1985.

Starche, Paula. "Airborne." *Concho River Review*, Spring 2014.

Wiggerman, Scott. "Easter in Texas." *Leaf and Beak: Sonnets*, Purple Flag, 2015.

Wilson, Steve. "Rondel: Willow at the End of Drought." *Poem,* November 2003.

Wilson, Steve. "Six Storms." *San Pedro River Review,* Spring 2016.

Other Anthologies from Lamar University Literary Press

A Shared Voice, Tom Mack and Andrew Geyer
The Beatest State in The Union, edited by Chris Carmona, Rob Johnson,
       & Chuck Taylor
Pushing the Envelope: Epistolary Poems, edited by Jonas Zdanys
The Great American Wise Ass Poetry Anthology, edited by Jerry
       Bradley and Ulf Kirchdorfer

For information on these and other Lamar University Literary Press
books, see www.lamar.edu/literarypresss

CONTENTS

Wind

Hot

Cold

Green

Introduction
Clay Reynolds

When I was a boy growing up in West Texas, or what we called "West Texas" (after all, it was west of Fort Worth), weather was part of our lives in the same way a poor relation might be, say an oafish uncle or unemployable cousin who moved in a long time ago and just wouldn't leave. Weather, to a kid in rural Texas, was a matter of consistent but paradoxically ever-changing inconvenience. We just accepted the weather, whatever it was. It was, as I said, like an unwanted relative: always there and usually in the way.

It's a commonplace in Texas to say something like, "If you don't like the weather, wait a minute. It'll change." That's not original to Texas, though. I've heard the same thing said about California and New England, Montana and Ohio, even in Florida, although it strikes me from my limited experience in "The Sunshine State" that there are really only two kinds of weather there—hot and wet—and both tend to occur at about the same time. Of course, the same could be said about parts of Texas, particularly down around the upper Gulf Coast—Beaumont down to Corpus Christi and for a considerable distance inland, although from time to time a cold snap may drift down that way and frost things up a good deal for a day or two, at least.

Even so, it's hard to talk about weather in Texas without talking about climate, which is a completely different thing, although they're often confused. Obviously Texas's raw size makes it a patchwork of environmental zones—"eco-systems" in climatologists' idiom. Only the "Big Island" in Hawaii matches Texas in the number and variety of eco-systems in a single state. In Texas, climate is commensurate with the state's sprawling geography: the high desert aridity of far West Texas extending from the mountain meadows of the western Pecos and upper Rio Grande valleys and high reaches of the Davis and Guadalupe mountains, where snow and ice are not infrequent guests, but also where salt flats and "walking dunes" of raw sand may be found, across the alkali flats of the Permian Basin, where dust-devils dance over flat, gritty desert and tumbleweeds make their indiscriminate way around a forest of cricket pumps, and on up into the flatlands of the *llano* past the breaks of the Double Mountain country and northward beyond the headwaters of the Prairie Dog Town Fork of the Red River, on and past Amarillo's "Golden Spread" and into the rich Canadian River valley and badlands of the Cimarron country, again where blizzards often occur and searing heat is an annual visitor. Throughout that region, surrealistic-appearing "wind farms" sprout huge tower-mounted propellers harvesting energy from the incessant and sometimes vicious streams of air that seem to rake the sky in all seasons. All of that is in sharp contrast to the more compressed ambiance that runs from somewhere between the Brazos and Trinity rivers northeastward to the sprawling grassy paddocks near Texarkana and Longview then down into the choking jungle thickness of the Big Thicket where cypress and loblolly and hardwood and palmetto compete for sunlight, breaking then westward toward an undulating steppe of verdant savannahs and rolling short-grass prairies of Texas's heartland. The hard-scrabble confusion of the Hill Country invites a kind of cross-section of sometimes wet-heavy over bone-dry ground that descends from up around Jacksboro near the Paluxy River over along the Caprock down through the cedar-cloaked Palo Pintos, then drops on to the liveoak and pecan groves along the Colorado and San Antonio and San Marcos Rivers, where it veers off to the southwest and flattens out to one of the most cruel and heat-choked deserts in the US, bisected only by the wavering Nueces and a labyrinth of rocky arroyos that appear to have never experienced moisture. And all of that descends then to The Valley, where some of the most fertile ground and brightest sunlight in the country is friendly to fecundity but harsh to humans. Then there's the Escarpment itself, jutting in a broken limestone line from the Rio Grande, north out of Uvalde and toward the leafy region around Kerrville and Junction and on up toward the Llano and Pedernales, the San Angelo and upper reaches of the San Antonio and San Gabriel rivers, a similarly thirsty and frequently hot region in summer, and a damper but cooler region in the fall and winter months. And that's not all of it, by any means.

One wonders, actually, where the early Anglo-American settlers were located when they first arrived in Texas and wrote back to their friends and families that the climate they found was "salubrious" and "a virtual heaven on earth." It certainly wasn't Laredo in the summertime or Dalhart in the winter or Odessa any time of the year.

It might be more accurate to say, actually, that in Texas, if you don't like the climate, move to a different part of the state. There are choices. Weather, though, isn't climate. Weather in Texas is, cliché or not, sudden and instantly changeable. It catches everyone, even multi-generation Texans, unawares; it'll kill you if you let it, especially if you don't respect it. Towering tornados and enveloping hurricanes and

14

pesky tropical storms that bring devastating winds and roof-crushing hail and inundating floods vie annually with rock-killing drought that reduces stock tanks and reservoirs to crusty fossil-dry vacancies and soul-freezing "blue northers" that blast out of the northern sky with a force that can steal the very life from man and beast and drop an icy shroud across the land. Sweeping dust-storms can be scouring the prairie like a sand-blaster while air so humid that it makes breathing a chore hangs over the dense swampy forests like a soused wool blanket that permits only mosquitoes to enter. Buzzards, hawks, and eagles will float on super-heated thermals over a parched prairie that bakes under a sky seared white by a blazing sun, while blinding snow storms coat the upper plains with an icy sheen that threaten anyone or anything in motion and will freeze dead anything standing still. Sometimes, all of these things can be happening at once.

Climate, then, may produce weather, but weather is what we remember.

My father loved to tell a story of how he was working on a windmill sometime in the 1930s. It was, he recalled, April 1—April Fool's Day—and was uncommonly hot. He said he and his brother were working under a scorching sun to replace a bent sucker-rod, when they saw the sky in the northwest turning dark behind rolling thunderclouds and towering anvils. Figuring it was an early spring storm, they rushed their work, but before they could finish, the cold front overtook them and the temperature dropped from somewhere around 90° to below freezing before they could scramble down from the windmill's tower. By the time they had fired up their Ford and were nearing "the house" (Texas parlance for home), it was hailing, then sleeting, then blowing snow. The dirt road beneath them turned to mud, then to ice, and when they finally slipped and slid to the barn where they parked the car, drifts had piled too high to get the rail-door open. He claimed that he and his brother could barely find the house in the blizzard swirling all around them. He also claimed that livestock and people froze to death in that norther that kept things frosty for more than a week.

I would never have called my father a liar, although I have to say that by the time in his life when this was to have taken place, he was working for the railroad, not doing ranch work, and I don't think his family owned a windmill, as they used a cistern for water for their horses and other stock. But the story illustrates the way in which weather is part of personal folklore, part of the heritage of being a

Texan. If you don't have a "weather tale" to tell, you probably "ain't from around here."

My parents both grew up during the Dustbowl, and I have no doubt that they saw weather that would make any modern person take quaking stock of his own mortality. I've seen films and photographs of huge dust storms, sometimes nearly a mile high (or so they were estimated) rolling out of the northwestern sky with a towering black wall of dirt that would soon coat everything with topsoil, blown, it was commonly said, all the way from Wyoming. Those storms *did* kill livestock—and people—and they left a legacy that existed well into my childhood. Our house when I grew up had all the windows painted shut, not to keep out heat or keep in cool but to keep dust from coating everything. I have, personally, witnessed dust storms bad enough to make streetlights come on at noon and to turn schools out early, and I've seen it "snow mud" when a cold front brought freezing temperatures and a wall of dirt all at the same time. And I've also witnessed thirty-degree temperature plunges when a norther raced down from the plains and turned a sun-broiled landscape frigid. Another cliché is to opine, "There's nothing between here and the North Pole but a bobwire fence—and it's down." That image is an easy one to conjure in any Texan's mind.

Naturally, you can't grow up in Texas without being aware of the potential violence of the weather. Tornados and lightning-laced thunderstorms are also part of my experience. My mother always spoke with some apprehension about "it coming up a cloud," which is how spring storms were characterized in those years before weather-service alarms and radar-measured warnings provided us with more accurate if less colorful vocabularies. Many houses in my neighborhood had storm cellars, which my family never used. "Only those with weak faith use storm cellars," my mother said. "You can't hide from God."

"Hide from God?" Are weather and God the same thing? At times, in Texas, one might think so. Standing out in the yard with my father and his "more faithful" friends and watching the angry clouds swirl and rotate overhead did provide me with a sense of wonder and of awe. In Sunday School, when we were taught about the Deity's destruction of Sodom or Noah's Flood, we all had a pretty good idea of what such a thing might look like. When we were presented with the forecasts of the Apocalypse in *The Book of Revelation*, I had no trouble envisioning the Four Horsemen riding viciously out of the massive wall of clouds of a blue norther, surrounded by the imps of Hell, flashing fire and horrific winds. I remember the scene in *The Ten Commandments* when Charlton Heston parted the Red Sea so the Children of Israel could escape Yul Brynner, and the Hollywood-animated clouds overhead twisted and ominously boiled and flashed. It looked like a fairly typical West Texas thunderstorm to me. God has nothing on the weather in Texas. If they aren't the same thing, then very likely even a vengeful God isn't nearly so scary. Religion offers redemption. Weather is unforgiving.

Heat, though, was more the weather I remember. Rain and cold and dangerous winds were too briefly experienced to loom large in my recollections. I grew up in the fifties, when there was a seven-year-drought. Elmer Kelton's most venerated novel, *The Time It Never Rained*, is named for that period. The common joke in that time went, "I do wish it would rain. Not so much for me. I've seen it. I'd just like for my children to have some idea of what it looks like." That was my period of youth, too. I honestly believed all grass naturally turned yellow around the first of June and stayed that way until the following April. Until I was about twelve, I never saw a creek or river I couldn't walk across, except when there was a flash-flood on the Red or the Pease, the result of heavy storms up in the Panhandle that would wash down and threaten the highway and railroad bridges with a torrent of sandy, salty water. At least twice, a major state highway bridge was totally washed away. But floods were rare, and those memories are more like a dream. On the whole, it was dryer than dry in those years. "Dry as a powder house," old-timers would say. "Dusty as a preacher's pocket," was another simile; so was "Dryer than a Republican's eye in an orphan's home." Too hot and too dry for chickens to lay, for cows to give milk, for anything to function right for long. Vegetation veritably crackled underfoot and trees drooped in the sun until their branches almost touched the ground. Those were the years when farmers pumped the water table down to critical levels and when dry-land farming ended, when ranchers sold cattle for pennies on the dollar, when the only thing that seemed to grow was Johnson grass, prickly pear, careless weeds, and the ubiquitous thorny mesquite. Those were hard years for a kid working on a farm or ranch or doing much of anything, like riding a bike, practicing school sports, or just being out of doors for any length of time—not that being indoors in those days before home air-conditioning was much better.

So weather was a constant in my life from the time I was born. It was never much of an obstacle to what passed for our ordinary lives, though. As Mark Twain so wisely noted, "Everybody talks about the weather, but nobody does anything about it." So heat or cold, wet or dry, we just worked around it, like the loutish, useless and unproductive houseguest it was, the weather sprawled out in our lives and offered very little in the way of help or consideration. It took food from our mouths, money from our pockets, and sometimes resolution from our purpose. About all that you could count on was that it would still be there tomorrow. In all those ways, come to think of it, the weather and God may well be the same thing.

Texans and Texas writers in particular take a perverse pleasure in talking about the weather and of working it into what they have to say about the state. Sometimes, I think they think they've discovered it, individually, and can't wait to tell people about it. One naturally considers the writing of the late Elmer Kelton in this regard, as I mentioned, but also the lyrical treatments of weather one finds in the stunning novels of R. G. Vliet, particularly *Solitudes*, which opens with the sudden violence of a blue norther contrasted with the sudden violence of man, or George Sessions Perry's *Hold Autumn in Your Hand*, where weather is more than merely a backdrop for the story, it seems to be a main character. When I think of writing and weather in Texas, my mind leaps to Dorothy Scarborough's famous and haunting novel, *The Wind*, where weather drives a woman mad in her isolation, or to William Owens' *Walking on Borrowed Land*, where weather and changes in it are so deeply engrained in the fabric of life that they are inseparable.

In my own work, weather is also a character, for I am as guilty as anyone of wanting to dramatize Texas weather and to lay claim to the uniqueness of my experience. In all of my books, particularly *The Vigil* and *Agatite*, I was particularly sensitive to what the weather was doing at any given moment in the stories. I also gave strong presence to it in *Monuments,* but it is always there in all my work, especially in some of my short stories, where the heat, cold, wind, and rain are always part of the situation, forming it and *in*forming it, making it, to me, more vivid, more real.

I am impatient with writers, mostly "outlanders" from elsewhere, who don't deal with Texas weather accurately. In large measure this is because they've never experienced it. Like social workers who are full of good advice for how to deal with recalcitrant and bothersome resident relatives but who have never had to share a sofa or dinner table with one, they try to imagine what it's like. Listen: You

18

can't do that, not if you want to make it real. It's not enough to say that it started to snow or rain. You have to experience it. You have to know what Texas heat feels like, how a blistering north wind, laced with ice and cutting through you like a knife can genuinely hurt. You have to have tried to walk or ride a bicycle or even a horse against a thirty-mile-an-hour gale, one that brings eye-stinging grit and superheated air that seems as if it's blowing out of Hell itself. You have to have seen hailstones the size of grapefruit and rain so laced with dirt that mud with the consistency of melted chocolate runs down a windshield and blinds you to the road. And you have to be aware that on any given afternoon, you can be fighting your way through drifts of snow, your head bent against an icy blast that seems to want to tear your very spirit out of your body, and then the next day, be setting fence posts and dripping sweat off your nose under a searing sun that feels like an super-heated anvil in a cloudless sky. In Texas, hardpan can turn to loamy bog in less time than it takes to say it, a stone-dry creek bed choked with dried-up weeds can become a raging torrent twenty feet deep in less time than it takes to think about it, a blue sky that is so translucent that it seems one might fall through it if one looked up too long can turn greenish-gray and nasty, bristling with lightning bolts and churning like an oceanic vortex overhead, sucking up trees and livestock and vehicles and whole houses into its angry maw, then spitting them out a county away, before one can turn around and run. A hurricane can uproot highways and unpin overpasses and change the shape of an entire coastline and a drought can cause concrete to buckle and sinkholes to open up and swallow buildings whole. Flood, wind, heat, cold: That's Texas weather in a short, sweet list.

You have to live that, and you have to learn to take it more or less for granted. I can always spot a native Texan when the weather changes rapidly. They're often merely amused by it. I remember attending one of my son's baseball tournaments in Burkburnett one hot, steamy summer evening. A storm was brewing off to the southwest—we could see it—and was seeming to approach. Suddenly a siren sounded and league officials were hustling everybody off the field and into the nearby gymnasium, as if in some misguided imagination, this would provide shelter. It was a regional tournament and I knew most of the people to be from elsewhere originally—"Yankees" in Texas parlance. They were visibly terrified. My son and I and a couple of other guys, though, Texans all, went up to the top of the bleachers to see what we could see. Sure enough, we spotted three individual twisters dancing off on the prairie, maybe ten or fifteen miles away, cast almost magically against a small slot of sunlight on the distant horizon. They weren't moving in our direction. There was no danger, although it was getting a somewhat damp from the edge of the storm's squall line that was raking the field. Still, it was an amazing sight, and it was beautiful. Some official was yelling at us to get down, come inside, to be safe. "Are you crazy?" he demanded. I shouted back that we were just fine—and sane, at least for Texans. We could see what was going on, and we were "living our faith," inasmuch as we realized that you can't hide from Texas weather. We also saw something that not very many people ever see. It was well worth getting a mite wet and wind-blown for.

I am not an idiot, though, contrary opinions to that statement notwithstanding. I know enough to come in out of the heat when it becomes too intense, to get down off a rooftop when lightning is in the vicinity, not to pitch a tent at the bottom of a downhill slope when rain threatens. I wear what I need to put on to insulate myself from the cold when it blows in. I've slipped and slid enough in winter to know that nothing's deadlier than Texans on ice, and I've nearly come to tears when I was so hot and thirsty and weary of turning another row to hoe and realized that it was only four o'clock and sundown was another half-day away. I've sat on tractor seats and prayed that thunderclouds in the distance would choose up sides and head my way to give the field I was plowing a good drenching and end my work week early, and I've shivered myself stupid at high school football games when the north wind was cold enough to frost-nip exposed ears and cause musicians' lips to freeze fast to steel mouthpieces. I know that weather in Texas is an unavoidable consequence of living here, and that, if I'm unhappy with it, all I have to do is wait a minute and it will change.

It's natural, then for Texans to incorporate weather into their writings, to adapt it to their characters and their stories, their poetry and their imagery. They want, after all, to "tell it," to try to capture it the way it was, the way it is. There's an element of "Texas brag" involved here. Excepting a few short weeks in the late autumn and a few short weeks in the early spring, weather in Texas is mostly intolerable. But Texans *do* tolerate it, and they want to brag about it. Nobody talks about "fair weather"; it's the hard stuff that attracts our notice; and, damn it, we want to brag about it, to "tell it." It's a hard thing to do, but writers understand that Texans' relationship to weather *is* as fundamental as their relationship to God, or to whatever spiritual commitment they may have. It cannot be avoided. It can only be endured.

But this is not an alarming problem. After all, if the weather at any given time is not to one's liking—and it almost never is—just wait a minute; it will change.

The poems and stories and essays in this volume all address weather directly. This is by design, and the poets and writers who have offered their visions and experiences and recollections of weather in Texas all do so against the backdrop of memory and sensations that have become part of the fabric of their lives. In some cases they focus on the weather itself—a storm, a seasonal change, a traumatic event, short or long term—and in some, they deal with the aftermath, particularly of hurricanes or tornados, floods or extended dry-spells. Some of these accounts are laced with fear and the panicked anxiety of the unknown fate that can come when the weather is violent and sudden, and in some they are colored by the stoical acceptance of the way things are and the way they're apt to be for some time to come. More often, though, they are infected with a sense of wonder, of awe, of the accepted if unrealized notion that, indeed, the weather *is* a lot like God.

A characteristic of this volume, though, illustrates that feature of Texas weather that encompasses the vastness of the state and the variety of climates that the geography dictates. From Jan Seale's finely wrought poetic and prose renderings about the weather of the lower Rio Grande Valley to Jim Hoggard's vividly reminiscent essay about the experience of racing a bicycle in the searing West Texas heat to Robert Flynn's wonderfully nostalgic Christmas tale to Dave Kuhne's ironic musings about the trials of a car-wash owner in the ever-changing Texas meteorological conditions, these writers seek to capture and then relate the intense and often intimate relationship individuals have with the weather.

In many ways, the poets in this volume, including the verse of the late Paul Ruffin and the always provocative and astonishing lines from William Virgil Davis, come closer to capturing the sensations that are associated with Texas weather, those that are connected directly to individual emotions and irrational responses and indelible memories. Carol Coffee Reposa's contemplative thoughts about the devastating but somehow mutable effects of a hurricane at Port Bolivar contrast against Karla K. Morton's verse assessments of the aridity of the Panhandle and Scott Wiggerman's sensual responses to the emergence of a carpet of wildflowers in the Texas Spring. Chris Ellery's whimsical recollections of his observation of dust devils dancing across the plains stand in relief against Sally Ridgeway's poetic account of the arrival of a norther on the coast and the recollections of drought that inform Steve Wilson's and Sherry Craven's poetic recollections evoke the brittle heat of a time when no one still believed in the promise of thunderstorms, a theme that is echoed in a mirroring prose work by Paul Ruffin. All of these works in this volume depict moments that have to be experienced but which are etched into the lives of any Texan, even an "outlander" like storm-chaser Jason Marc Harris, which become part of the fabric of what it means to be new in Texas and to experience Texas weather.

One remarkable commonality here, though, is how many of these works deal with rural Texas, be it a remote beachfront or open prairie or hard-scrabble farm. Only a few delve into the city life of Texas, so urbanized as it has become, where the destructive effects and sometimes horrific and sadly fatal results of Texas weather are so often revealed in the tragic aftermath. As a kid, I often heard it said of this town or that, in relation to its former glory and tragic fate: "Aw, it used to be something, but it got blowed away." This, I think, also speaks to the nostalgic sense of Texas weather, to the notion that the weather itself is tied in some way to the roots of all Texans, and that those roots run to farm and field, pasture and plain, sand and summit as much or more than they do to the concrete and steel of "Texas Urbana." After all, weather is as much about the land as it is about the people, and roots don't penetrate expressway and strip-center parking lots as readily as they do even the baked-over ground or brackish swamps of rural Texas.

In the end, though, it doesn't really matter whether one is in a West Texas wheatfield or standing in front of a Wal-Mart twenty miles from the Gulf. When it comes to the weather, the sky above an Alsup's in Seymour or a Lone Star Ice House in Poteet is no different from the sky above a Target in El Paso or a Starbucks in Dallas. A torrential flood in Lubbock is no less traumatic than overflowing bayou in Houston or a cresting river in San Marcos. Tornadoes have shown no more deference for Fort Worth or Wichita Falls than they have for Crowell or "Wide-Awake" Wylie. Weather has no respect for the pitiful erections and temporary scratchings mankind may have etched upon the land. It comes as it comes, and if humans, even Texans, are in the way, they can only ride it out, as they have no real say-so in the matter.

Beneath the words of all these pieces, though, what resonates the loudest is the notion that no matter what happens—weatherwise—we will, somehow, endure. Tomorrow, we know, the sun will once more rise over Texas, the wind will blow, the rain will fall, and heat and cold will come, each in its season. And everything will continue as it was, worn down a bit, for sure, and humbled, but somehow reassured that among all the things we know, the one thing we can always be sure of is the celestial mutability of the weather.

Dry

Rain Dance
Jan Seale

It's like this in Texas:
Get your hopes up

over high, silvercakey clouds,
finally climb out of the pool

go in rejoicing you made it
before the lightning struck

I say rejoicing 'cause
it's still a judgment of God
here in Texas

get dried off and think
of the irony
of being caught in the pool
when the thunderstorm hits
on the hottest day of the year.

Bring in the crying dog.

Close the windows at the first
nasty splats.

Thank God that breeze
is coming off the storm cloud

and then it's nothing.

It's you're under
the dress of the biggest mamma
in the circus. It's you're
with Poe in the pit.

It's you're in an iron lung
but too healthy for polio.

The clouds, they move
from east to west,
always just north of you.

The clouds, they belch a little
like a school boy on request.
The sun, it comes back grinning

like a satisfied lecher.
Cicadas wind up so sly
you don't know what it is
that's winding you up crazy,
standing, looking out the back door
at where it's not raining.

An Occasional Mermaid in Alpine

Jim LaVilla-Havelin

for Larry D. Thomas

while it may not be much of a
country for old men
Judd seemed to manage
pretty well, and you—
thriving in thin clear air and open
skies, awaiting, if only,
a mermaid to drop like the rain which
almost never comes, from a sky,
open enough to give her up.

Apache Creek, Near the Old Road

Joan Strauch Seifert

Gray hollows in the rocky swale
dotted with a shiny glint or two—water once was there.
Hanks of jimson-weed litter dusty ground,
scorning decent growth, dejected in their effort.

Land like this was never easy.
A sun-beast daily sears the flat miles merciless, proving that.

A buzzard swooping down onto an ancient deer path
takes no note if anything's alive.
He doesn't care; his feast will be somewhere there,
along the road that's his now.
And hundreds of mesquite trees, every spindly height and size,
crowd down the gray hillside like eager listeners
toward where the water was.

Listening for what? A long lost spring? A trickling sound?
Any hopeful sound.
And hearing none, nurture their harsh beans anyway.

Some things endure— mesquite trees, buzzards,
spirits of Kiowa braves wailing down deserted canyons,
miles, lifetimes away.

And store-fronts of the little towns that used to strive along this road?
Nailed shut, and crossed with weathered timbers.

Water

karla k. morton

Up in the Panhandle, it's all about the water.
Cattle gather at the prairie windmills
in hopes of a strong wind, for a good deep drink.

Shade is a luxury out there,
and the few trees that grow
have been planted by human hands

at rest-stops, or around houses—
nourished by bathwater and rain barrels
and yesterday's leftover iced-tea.

And when winter comes, they even grow thankful
for the bitter snow and ice,
which pierces the scrub and the sage—

knowing it will make its way
through each thawing level of dry earth,
back over to the stilled windmills;

the thirsty cattle, bellowing, beckoning the wind;
their short, furry ears, poised and waiting
for that first tiny squeal of metal against spinning metal.

The Snarl
Laura Quinn Guidry

The two grey foxes reappear at dusk.
They come for water from the makeshift
fountain and scraps of fruit we leave for them.
They know people live in the house

but knowing does not disturb their coming.
These two are likely from last spring's litter.
This is the month the mother would've
snarled and sent them away.

Drought has drained life from the pond.
Evergreens have turned brown, brittle.
Not far away, wildfires rage.
We sniff the air for smoke.

Mother has bared her teeth.

August: Carmine, Texas
Laura Quinn Guidry

Wildflowers that came in waves have gone.
Cattle scruffy as the ground they graze.

Three dogs, gone feral, kill and eat a calf. A frog,
while being swallowed by a snake, cries like a kitten.

After weeks of drought, a storm shatters the air.
Rain, too much too fast, to nourish.

Above the trees, hawks and turkey buzzards
scan earth for the living and the dead.

One could roam around in a haze of heat
but that would be a mistake.

Thirst

Laura Quinn Guidry

I wish I'd set out this tin
bucket to catch all
the moments that rained
down, then ran
off in rivulets or the sun burned
away before they'd had
a chance to soak into the ground.

If I'd thought to do that then,
now I could reach
down with this knocked-about
metal cup and bring up a sip.
It would taste of gladness.

Buffalo Sun
Lawrence Welsh

only burning sage
creosote
salt cedar:
the silver feathers
in smoke
as portraits
of camouflage:
they see a hide
and seek
a coming on
until the sun calls
becomes its name

Dry Lightning
Mike Baldwin

tears the air asunder—
a too-bright, jagged crack of light—
then the thunder,
blundering among flat-topped Texas hills,
announcing the arrival
of a green-black grumbler,
turning dusk to darkness,
roiling and rumbling,
threatening and promising,
but then passing, unpausing,
carrying an entire lake of water
elsewhere tonight,
leaving us somehow
unworthy of its wet blessing.

West Texas Drought
Paula Starche

When it rained in the Fifties
we opened the windows and doors
huddled at the threshold
and peered out. Then Mom

stood outside on the open porch
smelling wet earth. We ran
around in circles kicking up damp dust.
Sticky little frogs hopped on our palms
and squished under our soles.

I hear the rain this morning
heavy to the south moving northeast.
I want an accounting.

Candle Moths Drawn to Hot and Dry at the Ranch in July

Sherry Craven

The summer we needed rain, the candle moths came,
a time of soul-reckoning. They took over the days
like the curse of a black plague, covering our sofa
and bed and arms and food with their brown fuzz bodies.

Moving all night the furry creatures flew into the food,
blindly they crept under pillows and blankets, into
shoes, fluttering in kitchen drawers, their beating wings
shivered the towels in our bath, making my heart quiver
like the flame of the candles we lit in defense.

Kerosene, bucket and lamp ballast on the dining table
in hopes the moths would hurl into a drowning fate,
to lure them into a pail for a grave. The old-timers said
it was due to no rain, the heat and the drought, their looking

for respite and light to navigate their way and finding our lone house
on its own amidst 30 sections of barbed wire and pasture, a beacon.

They left us suddenly and eased my apocalyptic fears
except for the knowledge of how easy they died,
a bucket of kerosene for a grave.

I looked at the 30 parched sections of land dotted with
lime green mesquite and black Angus here and there,
stretching far beyond what my eyes could take in and thought
of the candle moths with nowhere to hide and it seemed
a fair justice. We all have a tendency to follow the light.

Rondel: Willow at the End of Drought
Steve Wilson

Willow against a night sky. Its first few leaves, a hesitant green
  in the still-cool dark of March. By late summer, the branches—long
  and low, heavy with heat—would spread a canopy of shade along
the walk. Other trees pull back then. They take the hard months lean

to last, riding out the dry spells. This one, though, like droughts we'd
        seen
  in schoolbooks. Dead rivers. Whole fields brown and brittle. Cattle
        gone.
  Willow against a night sky. Its first few leaves, a hesitant green
in the still-cool dark of March. By late summer the branches, long,

had dropped their leaves and done. The world grew keen
  with thirst, the air. . . a dead haze, full of white light and drawn
  taut. "Rain don't come soon, we may have to move on."
Nearly forgotten: the promise of clouds, the old song of rain in the
        ravine.
Willow against a night sky. Its first few leaves, a hesitant green.

Burial Weather

Ysabel de la Rosa

for JHC

The parched earth breaks, forming fissures.
Thunder comes tumbling from on high.
Stretching-cracking-splitting sounds fall
on us, roll through us, unaccompanied
by lightning or rain

I need you.

Your body lies beneath the ground-up
baked-dry red flour of this land,
this place now
so emptied that
not even sky

not even sky can cry its
beneficial tears, nor I, who stand
beneath the pouring-down
light, the bearing-down heat,
feeling the thunder in my bones,
staring, numb, into the summer sun

Storm
Paul Ruffin

From about ten o'clock on, a cell blossomed steadily in the south, beyond the hill, building on itself until it stood one thin column of cloud, with the slightest orange mushrooming at the tip. The two of them, a man and a woman well into middle age, leaned in on the hoes in their small, dusty garden, now so chastised by long days of sun and dry winds that there seemed little need in bothering to care for what few things remained alive. The beans were thin and pale, the squash wilted, tomatoes stunted. Little swirls of dust rose as they went back to their hoeing, reaching out and dragging bright blades, burnished by daily use and sharpened to half their original length, just beneath the soil crust. Sprigs of grass fell over and wilted almost immediately in the blasting sun.

"How can you tell it's a thunderstorm so soon," she asked after he had commented on it the third time, "and not some ordinary cloud?" She had stopped again and stood, propped on the hoe, watching the southern sky.

He turned from his hoeing beside her to say, "Because of its shape, behavior, the way it is updrafting."

She leaned and took a swipe at a patch of green. "It looks like some kind of flower, about to break out in color."

"That's the cumulus stage we're watching," he continued, "just sits there updrafting through the chimney, drawing moisture, developing the cell."

"Is it raining under it?" Sweat was beginning to seep into her eyes at the corners.

"No, just the opposite right now—sucking up moisture, like a kitchen sponge."

She reached her sleeve across and wiped the sweat away. "I wish someone would squeeze it out here, where it or one of its brothers has been sucking up our moisture for weeks on end, not returning a drop to use."

He hoed on in silence for a while, then answered, "Well, someone will get rain later, somewhere, when the cell's matured on up in the day, probably over around Livingston, where they don't need it."

After lunch they climbed to the top of the hill that rose from the edge of their back yard and sat under an oak to watch the storm. Behind them their square little house sat boldly in white at the edge of the browning pastures that stretched out from the foot of the hill and ended at the dark green border of the creek, which always managed a trickle in the harshest of droughts. A handful of lean cattle worked their heads in and out of the brush at the creek edge, and a spiral of buzzards turned lazily above them, drifting along with the wind.

A stranger passing where they sat would have remarked that what he looked down on had to be one of the sorriest East Texas farms he had ever seen: small, drought-parched, poorly fenced, outbuildings faded and flimsy, the house so small that passage from the front to back door could be made in five good bounds. And he would have wondered what could keep two people out here, in obvious poverty, to battle with the inimical forces of nature when there must be better lives for them somewhere else. And certainly there were better farms to be had.

But they would not have cared what he said. They were there by choice, gave up affluent lives in the city, walked away from a world of options, preferring a life of stark simplicity. They were products of the sixties, free spirits, he with a braided tail of hair yet, though it was streaked with gray, and she a lean, weathered woman whose arms and legs were knotted with hard muscles, her face ravaged by sun and wind. And the farm, pitiful as it might be, was theirs, paid for, and it satisfied them. That was what mattered. They were who and where they wanted to be, though they had long since—and with great pleasure—eschewed the foggy world of drugs and eastern philosophies and open social protest. They never regretted their retreat to the country, except when nature, in one of her malevolent streaks, countered every move they made.

The storm was thickening now and beginning to boil with what she supposed looked like anger, if a storm could be angry or nature could be unkind.

"There seems to be an unfairness about all this," he said quietly, "the way the sky takes away our water day after day and carries it off to someone else, who we do not know and who may not even need it."

"There's a balance in things, I guess." She watched while the top of the storm flattened out like hair whipping out from a girl's head. She could feel a freshening in the air from the direction of the storm, a stirring of her long brown hair. There were times like this, when she sat in silence and watched the changing face of the sky, that she imagined what their children would have been like, had they managed to have them: the boys tall and lean like their father, with feathery brown eyes

40

and skewed smiles, the girls like her, willowy and pretty in a plain way, hair fine as smoke. But she did not allow herself to wander long in the sky, stopping always short of the precipitous plunge into aching emptiness.

He pointed: "That's the anvil forming on top. The storm's fatter and darker now, and you can tell which way it's moving by the anvil."

"Which way do you think it's moving?" she asked, not in challenge.

"Away from us, off to the west, but I would have known that anyway, without the anvil."

"You're being cynical again. It may come back." He had in recent years developed a darker side than she had ever known him to have; he smiled less. She worried about it sometimes. Once in one of his foul moods, brought on as usual by extended dry weather, he declared he was ready to give it all up and move back to the city. "I feel so incredibly earthbound," he had said, driving his boot heel down onto the dry, hard soil. "Dark, earth-colored, like a corpse turned back into clay." But she coaxed him out of his despair, loving and reassuring him as she always had. Still, the moods came so sudden on him now, and so often.

"Let's get some more rows done." He picked up his hoe and started back down the hill, turning to look once more at the widening storm. "Somebody is really getting a shower." He pointed to the dark streaks under the belly of the storm. "A solid curtain of rain."

They hoed on in the midafternoon heat until he shaded his eyes toward the sun and announced it was time for other chores.

"Before we get on with other things, can we rest?" she asked him as they walked to the barn. It was not that she was really tired. The work would always be there, whenever they turned to it, the cycle of chores as endless as the seasons, so she felt no urgency, no compelling haste. That was the attitude they had agreed on in the beginning, and she had kept the agreement.

"Sure," he told her, "why don't we watch other folks get rain?"

She pointed up to the loft. "Let's go up there." They lay then across the bales of hay and looked out to the south, where the storm was grumbling and tossing about. Years earlier what happened next would have been as predictable as sunrise, but now they merely lay side by side, touching each other but without passion, like two shoes set in a closet.

41

"It's already dispersing," he pointed out, "see how the black is fading out of it?"

"It seems closer."

"Seems but isn't," he said. "Just wider and taller."

"It *sounds* closer," she persisted. The curtain of rain seemed to be drawing toward them, the trees whipping and thrashing along the creek, the sun fading. "I believe that it is going to rain on us."

For an answer he slid off the hay and backed down the ladder. "Well, I don't," he told her as he started off down toward the pasture bottom. "You stay up there where you can be dry, if you believe that it's going to rain. I've got to go check the fence down there where the bull broke through last week."

She watched him cross the pasture, a weak shadow rippling alongside him and slightly behind like some pursuing ghost, and disappear into the brush that bordered the creek just as the sun darkened and a solid curtain of rain slid across the hill. He burst out of the green wall when the rain reached him, his hands out and spread to the flashing, rumbling sky, as if he would gather in the whole storm. The barn roof drummed with heavy drops, then roared. The last she saw of her husband before the storm swallowed him, he was running in wide circles, his face aglow, hair trailing straight out behind, arms spread like some enchanted boy trying hard to fly.

Wet

Lightning in the Pasture
Carolyn Dahl

Cattle are the gentle clocks of the ranch, but this morning, they
bellow with strain, show unwillingness in their stance, a contrariness

of horns though we offer a treat of oats. Yesterday, digging
fence posts, we had to flee the field and run for the nearest shed

when a sudden storm struck. We had no time to bring the herd
home to protection as duty required. Driven by instinct to seek

the shelter of trees, fifteen gathered under the oaks, unaware
lightning can travel through a tree's roots. The cattle put their faith

in the solidarity of ground. When the lightning bolt struck,
we saw them flash brilliant before collapsing on charred hooves.

Unborn calves ejected from their mother's wombs, unfinished.
Some exploded, their parts caught in branches. We had

named them all. The storm didn't care. Today our four
survivors chew their cuds hard and fast, as if rumination

were a way through grief. We've given up on reasons,
or the question of how to replenish the herd. We walk

among them, rub their singed fur, watch them chew.
Hoping burned grass will eventually turn to a pardon.

Signs
Alan Birkelbach

If we'd listened we might have heard
some dread crows warning us.
If we hadn't been so full of sleep we might have seen
the sun come up behind black and green clouds.

Our horses, somehow, saw it coming first,
and tried to steer us home but too late then!
A slate-gray sky came down
and exploded on us with a sudden rush.

We closed our mouths and bent our heads
but that wind turned each seam and hidden fold.
Our boots turned into buckets.
Our brims fell flat against our eyes.

So we decided: we breathed once, deep,
then yee-hawed it, yipped and roared,
threw our heads back, foolish, daring,
slapped the reins, and cheered our horses to lather, set for home,

and laughed at all Fates that would drown us,
and washed ourselves with sopping bravado,
our horses' prints washing away in the mud
even as they were stamped.

We were cavalry leading a hopeless charge,
fearless of the spears of rain, the missiles of hail,
laughing and cursing that we hadn't scried the thunder,
but still looking up to read the twisting entrails of the sky.

Gray Descending
Bryce Milligan

On 281 North

Today I take to the highway knowing
that this time no home waits ahead.

Befriending gray descends, comforting all
the dry cracked lands when drought-wracked streams

seem to swell as rain-scent enchants the plain.
Today I take to the highway

to sing of rain, the great gray gift that turns
these tawny pastures green again.

Ahead, gray descends, befriending all but
the ones who cannot see beyond

its dim and misty shroud. Today I take
to the highway to weep alone,

to weep aloud, knowing her hands are still,
cold, and gray. Ahead, gray descends,

befriending those who shun blue sky and sun.
Today I take to the highway.

Valley Summer Storm
César de Léon

It doesn't need a reason
but itself,
to breathe,
to arrive unannounced
smelling like the beach
with an aftertaste of
cotton fields that
are not ready to be
picked until late August
under a mad sun.

Storm's A-Coming
Diane McMeans Kreger

"Storm's a-coming," Granny Mac said softly as if to herself, never breaking the rhythm of her pea shelling. The purple hulls plinked into the pan nestled in the folds of her apron as she gently rocked—back and forth.

"Yes sir-ee. Gonna rain." This came a second later from Aunt Jeffie. Her movements mimicked those of her sister; they had shelled peas and snapped beans on this porch since they were young girls.

As I pressed my nose against a section of the screened porch to gaze out at the blazing sun beating down on the garden rows stretched out in front of us, I almost said, "Oh, it's not going to rain." But I swallowed that impulse quickly; Granny Mac was never wrong, especially when it came to the weather... and money and love and heartbreak.

Before long, the wind picked up, and the chickens started moving from the shade of the big oak, heading toward the barn. *Tha-wack! Tha-wack!*

"Little Sister, git the latch," Granny Mac said firmly. I crossed the porch to grab the screen door as it made one more "slap" with the flow of the breeze. Just as I secured the latch, the rain splatters started—each drop making a little funneled hole in the dirt before the ground darkened with moisture. *How did they know*? I pondered, watching the rain quicken.

Granny Mac always knew! On that summer day long ago deep in the Piney Woods of East Texas, I had no way of knowing that, over the years, Granny's words would echo in my head. There would be many times that I would hear her soft words within the silence of my thoughts —*Storm's a-coming,* and most of the time it had nothing to do with the weather.

A Trinity Flood

Jeffrey DeLotto

Fort Worth, Texas
May, 1876

We were digging clams down in the Trinity River
Bottom just north of Ayres' place, half a mile east
Of Sycamore Creek, had us a couple dozen, my
Sister Iola and me, even busted two open on a rock,
The hand-sized shells thick with mother of pearl,
The meat big as a chicken egg, we chewed and
Swallowed the muscle and other guts, the first
Fresh meat we'd had since Uncle Joe brought us
That calf one of his heifers dropped in April dead.

The morning was still and cook-pan hot off the
Mud and sand of the riverbed, two bleached
White buffalo skulls staring from the southern
Cut bank, washed down no doubt from a spilled
Wagonload north of town, and we hadn't paid
Any mind to the empty blue sky until a rattle
Of cottonwood leaves told of a breeze. The jack
Oaks down to high water line, their thick roots
Reaching out of the sand like down turned fingers,
Kept us from seeing, but once up on the higher
Ground, dragging our croaker sacks through thorn
And low-draped mustang grapes, we saw the north
And west horizon frowned up thick as smoke with
Storm clouds, a cool breeze swept our sweat-pointed
Hair off our brows and half-way home, the clear
Robin's egg sky not yet gone from the south,
It started to come down.

Eight days it rained, eight days and eight nights,
Almost straight through it came down, more than
Just a rain but like a being, an old beast crouching
Over us, sometimes a sprinkle, sometimes a drum-
Roll roar so hard and loud the shingles sounded like
They'd bounce off the roof....and she came out of her

Steep cut banks without hesitation, like milk welling
Out of a bottle filled by a distracted hand, like milk
Washing out almost oily onto a table, spreading past
Trees, around houses, over streets, picking up the
Dust and straw and forgotten tins and sacks, rising,
Heavy like spilled milk, like that thick brown milk
Grandmama sometimes made me on Saturdays after
Papa went out to harness the team, with bitter old coffee
From the stove and some sticky blackstrap, but I swear
I will never savor such stuff again.

A day after the rain blew by, that river moved over our
Town, more than two miles flooded out past Richland,
That dirty water moved sometimes more like a bank
Of cloud than something to loathe, until you saw the
Cows and pigs and more come bobbing by, all bloated
Out, hooves poking up like overturned table legs, until
The water crept back, leaving roads long, shiny smears,
Like tracks of mucus down some sick child's lip—
And I heard more that one man ask, not the last time
In coming days, what in hell were we doing here.
But after day nine and the sun shown down bright,
Clear, our world washed and clean, we all hung our
Clothes and linen and mattresses out on fences to dry.

After another three days the river dropped back down
Into her banks and we started seeing them, the animals
And the caught folks. Already we had some laid out,
From their houses, found in their haylofts, old Ephraim
Humphrey, Frank Forney, Colonel Henry Granger, and
Put them in the ground quick in the sticky heat, shovels
Sticking on every swing in the muck, the soaked shrouds.
But those others down closer to the Trinity, caught
In trees, one man's leg trapped beneath his wagon seat,
The whole rig bogged half-way up the bank, just hanging
There in the bright sun after the water fell back, the broken
Singletree wedged in the mud, swollen, Lord Jesus, and
The flies...and then what we found, Billy Spurlock and
I, found caught up an old rock wash where all those big
Old limestone snail shells, ribbed and an easy foot across

Kept us thinking about this book by some man named
Linnaeus Colonel Smith loaned me....I just caught a spot
Of red, thought it a cardinal I did, until the blue-white
Dimpled arm told me what she was, maybe washed and
Rolled downstream from some house in Hell's Half Acre
We had heard about, by the look of her scarlet dress and
Stockinged foot, we never did know, but me and Billy,
Before we told a soul, pulled her out, I swear we feared
She'd come apart, and her red dress and underclothes
All twisted up around her waist, and her legs like fresh
Dressed hams fell open, and we stared and stared, looked
At each other and stared again at...the woman of her,
The mystery, the way it was all inside, and we couldn't
See, and we were all outside, all on the outside, always.
We fixed her back, swore secrecy and found our folks
And put her up there outside Ayres' Cemetery with so
Many others, Mama saying Mama's sure that woman
Is in a better place, but I kept quiet.

Now, as we roll and steam into the twentieth century,
My practice, Evangeline, the children doing well, Billy
Down in Austin and us with a new courthouse and college
And rail yards and all, everyone is saying that a golden
Day is upon us, but I see that old Trinity snaking down
There in the clay, I recall a lost soul who showed herself
To a stranger, and I am not so sure.

How the Body Heals
Katherine Hoerth

What else could you do but begin your grieving,
weep for all the branches the storm had snapped in
two, the oak tree dripping with loss, the windblown
fence that was leaning

to the sodden soil, lantanas lying
supine underneath all the weight of water
drowning like you drown every day in your pain. But
this is how healing

comes—it simply happens. Let crows devour
what no longer lives, the disease. Let fire
ants march off with pieces of petals. Let the
roots find their strength to

try again, to snake through the ground like nerves through
skin, through flesh, through bone. Let them swallow
rain, let pain evaporate like a puddle in the
sunshine, a droplet

at a time. Let vines overcome the fallen
fence, unfurl their leaves like new skin, their flowers
flush with life and pollen. Let nature have her
way. Let the wind wash

off the scent of dying. Let bones reset, muscles
flourish, strength return like the hummingbirds in
autumn. Let it happen again, your body
thrumming with healing.

Visitor

Laura Quinn Guidry

When I raise the window shade
a grey fox, the color of morning,
ambles away. Rain comes down hard
after five months. Thunder cracks.
Clocks flash. A window leaks.
We mop up with towels, retire
to the den to watch a video.
Rain pelts the metal roof, eases.
Stop the movie, you say. *Come see this.*

A pileated woodpecker has landed
in the oak closest to the house.
Uncommon, wary bird, big as a crow,
back as black, crested with red feathers
tall and thick like hair. White-faced,
the black line off its eye is like a mask,
the line off the base of its bill
turns downward as in a grimace.
A jester, a mad clown.

Not exactly pretty, you remark.
Better than pretty, I say.
The bird ratchets the tree
and is gone. Its call rises
to a wild laugh. Then, in the clearing,
we see the wide, white underwing
gleaming like the moon
beneath storm clouds.

Disturbance

Patrick Allen Wright

I like to hear
low peals of thunder,
watch swaying oaks,
smell impending rain,
count seconds
between flash and roar.

There—six seconds—
six miles.
A Burger Chef box
blows across the asphalt.
The first drop strikes
surprisingly large.

Downtown Downpour

Priscilla Frake

The clouds ripple on grids of silver, tossed
between canyon walls: Louisiana
and Polk. The streets below are slots of noise
and asphalt, where red lights wink in shadow.
I feel small as a microbe, picking my way
down Smith. This is the rabbit hole, the wrong
end of a telescope, where things grow smaller

and more remote. I see the sky only
in echoed reflections and feel the earth
through soles of pavement and hear the bayou
move in a cage of concrete and then the storm
floods me to the quick. There is no distance
between street and sky, between city and skin,
between self and tempest, when it rains.

August Rain Melancholia
Robin Scofield

Small white feathers
see-saw down from the pines.
The nestlings prick
with new bristly feathers
after the molt of their down.
This generation to the next—
when it's time to fledge—
they'll be ready, rain or not.

They fall and take
flight at the same time
like a new born idea.
Under the fallen needles,
I find good dirt. I move
them and make a path
in sand. Under the flowering
bush, the dung beetle doesn't
filter what's good
from what's bad.
He turns it all the same.
He scrabbles away
from me, in case
my shadow be
a danger. Hard to tell
whether to go on a walk,
half the sky sunny and
half dark, half the sky
silent, half muttering.
I stay close to home,
feeling electric.

The Way It Is On the Gulf Coast

Sandi Stromberg

Dawn drives in
on a blue sky.
Heat pushes in the clutch,
wisps of white clouds
accelerate to
cumulus, darken.
And thunder revs up
its grand prix engine.
The wind shifts
into overdrive.
Ginger stalks
bend deep and swirl
as drops ram
the obstinate
ground, the
windows, the roof.
Minutes pass.
Streets choke.
Then, silence
as gears slip
into neutral.
Water trickles
into a bayou.
Dusk makes a clean
sweep of the sky.
The road clears
for sunset.

Six Storms
Steve Wilson

Storms flower, the skies
blackening to slate. Nightjars
dive into an echo.

***

Rain thunders in, all teeth and bone.

***

Autumn storms conjure
a second spring—
fall greens, flowers,
in spite of itself.

***

Under lowering skies, summer
growls and glowers, then goes.

***

—the eloquence of mist at storm's edge—

***

storms
descended—evening
all day

Opacity on Ranch Road 12
Vanessa Couto Johnson

When the rain like soft needles
aiming into my windshield

tests this car's health, the road
is a wet darkness ahead.

Reflections amplify this sightlessness.

A doe gently paces its neck
into range and we both become
polite avoidance. This manner

is instinctual. Hours earlier,
a vulture crossed the air
above a street and I slowed
into lateness. What if we touched.

Driving is not a contact sport.

Whenever you have had me
follow, your tail-

lights are easily divisible from
me. I prefer to write a list
of turns. If I am the silver ball
in the maze, let me be the hand, too.

The rain still stinging glass,
I go down a hill and find
a large man ascending on

the road's white line. His pale
shirt wet, elbows acute.

I deflect enough, hoping
my motion speaks to the one
vehicle behind me as well,
and then the language ends there.

Titans of North Texas
Jason Marc Harris

To avoid raising any false expectations here, let me just say, this story doesn't involve sports, and I wasn't born in Texas. I haven't even lived here a full two years. So what business do I have submitting a story about Texas weather? Aside from having one relative back in the Nineteenth Century who was a Texas Ranger (so now you've got to pay attention), let me tell you, I've got some weather perspective: I grew up my first eighteen-years in the dry triple-digit heat of the Sacramento Valley of California, yet saw my first funnel cloud out there in the Sierra foothills of a March day. I've lived four-years in Florida and watched the rain pour down over twenty inches in two days from Tropical Storm Fay, and I spent six years up in Seattle, Washington—the first twelve months so laden with purplish-grey clouds that I hungered for blue sky as that year set some kind of sequential record for overcast in Puget Sound. I lived another six years in the Midwest, where I've fallen on my ass twice from slipping on black ice in Ohio, and—too eager to slide down on a trash can lid on a local sledding hill—I've skidded off a snow-covered road in Michigan, as I was coming too fast around a sly curve. Also while in Michigan, I hitched myself to a group of veteran storm chasers, and thanks to their skills while driving from Kansas to Iowa, I saw about ten tornadoes back in 2008. So, I've learned a few things about what the weather can do, be it how a thunderstorm's mesocyclone sinks so low it can drag a dusty wall cloud across a farmer's field and crack a concrete silo in half when that sand-and-hay choked tornado blasts though, or how sometimes you've got to run the damn wipers at the same time as the defroster during squelching humidity on the Space Coast of Florida. By the time I came here to Texas, I was ready for the Lone Star State's multifarious mighty weather. Ready as one can be, right?

I've seen the mountains of Southwest Texas and Hill Country: the peaks and ridges of Big Bend, sprawling brown and grey blooms of rock and dust that tower over the shallows of the Rio Grande, and like many Texans I've climbed up the steep slope of Enchanted Rock, which hides "fairy shrimp" in freshwater puddles. Having visited Death Valley in California I can see the parallels of these ancient arid ranges and ravines. In Big Bend, I've watched roadrunners and coyotes scuttle and lope along both gravel and asphalt roads while cars clanked and hissed by. But the biggest billowing most dynamic shapes I've seen in Texas are a vanishing range of titanic proportions up north near the Red River—bubbling cumuliform clouds, surging into deep layers of hazy dark blue. I've watched those anvils mushroom and drift and seen those dragging bulks of low-based storm bellies twist into blurry horseshoes of hail and wind. At night, I've stood on the rickety deck and marveled at "spider lightning" or "anvil crawlers"—lightning that wriggles beneath thunderheads, braiding horizon-to-horizon with dazzling incandescence.

Now, like I said, I'm new to Texas, so I don't have a lifetime of experience with weather in the Lone Star State. However, because I've moved around a lot and have also had some experience as a mobile storm spotter and chaser, I've got a unique perspective to share on the atmosphere around here, how it compares, and what it dishes out. You hear folks say in the Midwest, "if you don't like the weather, wait five/ten/fifteen minutes"—you hear the same thing in Florida and right here in Texas. You sure don't hear that in California or Washington. While Texas at times can pull in that dry air that blows from the West over the Rockies, there's also the swampy bay called the Gulf Coast—with fire-water seething northward, which builds up some serious wind shear, humidity, and meteorological drama, that's for sure. Especially in the Spring.

Last May I joined a friend of mine, Michigander by birth, Matt Bridgewater, and together we headed north May 15th to Wichita Falls to get in position for the High Risk outbreak that the Storm Prediction Center had announced. Meteorologists also forecast that the high probabilities of large and dangerous tornadoes would lure storm chasers internationally to the plains, and that the numerous chasers could contribute to traffic snarls on narrow "primitive" roads.

The storms didn't end up quite living up to their forecast hype of dominating the vast expanse of plains all the way into Kansas and Nebraska. Also, since I value honesty above suspense, Matt and I did not end up seeing tornadoes that day. We picked the strongest storm, which later produced a tornado, but we didn't get to see it because we elected not to punch through a core of baseball-sized hail and end up on precariously "primitive" roads. Nevertheless, there was plenty of excitement, and a grand immersion into Texas weather. Up close and personal. Even without a shattered windshield or busted side-mirror.

When we showed up at the hotel on the outskirts of Wichita Falls, there were no obvious signs that night of the drama in the sky that would unfurl over Northern Texas the next day. Aside from a few wisps of cloud, the air felt dry. Indeed, a dryline was setting up a hundred miles or so to our West, and destined to be overtaken by the burst of moisture streaming from the Gulf the next day.

The room itself was simple: two beds, a closet, a bathroom—whose ceiling was partly crusted with dark mold, so peculiarly formed in v-shaped flecks that they resembled long-bodied termites, complete with filmy hints of wings. An indication of the cloying humidity that more typically occupied the room? Perhaps so.

Morning brought us the feeblest of passing rain showers, which was a promising step because you don't want the atmosphere to be worked over before the big show gets going. The sun soon was back out, evaporating those sprinkles, and promising to make things muggy quickly. Matt and I checked the online updates to the day's explosive weather forecasts, but at the bare bones continental breakfast, we learned that due to the hotel's policies, we had to switch the television back to Fox News rather than the Weather Channel. Thus, we relied on weather apps for our smartphone, tablet, and laptop, as would be the case throughout the day, except where coverage failed because of spotty networks—an inevitable pitfall while chasing storms.

After checking out of the hotel in Wichita Falls, we hit the road and picked a feasible spot to await the birth of storms. Based on the weather models' predictions of where the lower and mid-level jets of winds were supposed to really pump up in the afternoon, we positioned ourselves to be ready to travel west or south, choosing a base of operations close to the Oklahoma border at a McDonald's in Vernon, Texas. The Golden Arches afforded us not only free wireless and cheap food but was conveniently located near a good paved network of roads, such as Highway 287, which we had already taken west from Wichita Falls, and which we'd soon follow to Quanah, but also we had access southwest via 70.

Although we were the first chasers on scene at McDonalds, once we got ready to leave, we discovered two huge SUVs out in the parking lot, both with wind gauges and other equipment on the roof. The bigger of these chase vehicles was prominently labeled as the "Storm Warn Unit" and proclaimed itself as a "Minuteman" vehicle focused on "disaster response." As we later learned online, these well-outfitted chasers were inspired to self-organize after the devastation that struck Joplin, Missouri, in 2011. It was interesting to see these heavy-duty pieces of machinery committed to the same fast-food base of operations that Matt and I were now preparing to leave.

Isolated supercell storms fired up on radar. Time for an intercept. A couple storms—one of them already tornado-warned—had developed too far west to get to feasibly. However, a third storm approached rapidly from the southwest. We could see the broad shield of the anvil unfolding across the sky. Quanah looked to be a perfect spot to stop and watch this storm pass by without overtaking us. You want to stay ahead of the storm, aiming ideally to get a view of the southwest quadrant where the rotating part of the supercell would manifest a potential funnel.

We drove west on 287 to Quanah, while the thunderstorm loomed ever larger—the cauliflower-textured overshooting top no longer visible as the anvil had blocked our angle of view, and the lower and mid-level clouds thickened and darkened. As we closed in on Quanah, we could see the base of the storm and a bowl-shaped lowering—the wall cloud, from which a funnel might soon begin to form. We took a turn north on Highway 6, turned slightly west, and pulled into Quanah High School's parking lot off Hillcrest Drive.

Although trees partly blocked the view to the west, as well as power lines, houses and businesses, we glimpsed the wall cloud's ragged edges: frayed fingers of moisture dipping downwards, but not circulating. Ahead of the storm, a shelf cloud pushed northeast with its fluffy yet steep ridge or prow.

We got out of the van and witnessed a couple white bolts of cloud-to-ground lightning to the west strike near that wide-based frayed-fingered vase-like feature—the wall cloud, which signaled where the storm sucked in warm moisture beneath the coal-black and seaweed-green clouds that promised a hail core in the vicinity as well. The thunder wasn't close enough to alarm us, but the storm was losing our interest.

The storm looked a bit mushy in its middle and the anvil lacked the striations that often indicated crisper and more significant development. However, there was a clear-slot behind the wall cloud, which often presages the storm is organizing general rotation, but we did not witness any visible rotation. Soon, the business-end of the storm drifted out of view to the north. It was high time we repositioned to get ready to see a couple more candidates for tornado genesis.

We got back to 287, heading towards 6, but we pulled over to set up our cameras pointed across a field with a fine view of the southwest. Another wall cloud drooped from the next storm that appeared to be mimicking the previous storm's trajectory. White veils of hail hung near

64

the wall cloud. The distance was just too far to make out any significant movement in terms of circulation amid those ragged tendrils.

Other chasers had pulled over along 287 and had set up their tripods—some of them had preceded us, and along about 1/4 mile of highway you could see these metallic companions to severe weather photographers. Camera tripods stood planted amid tall prairie grass. All that metallic equipment perched like wading birds, as though Sandhill Cranes had gained the art of metallurgy, clad themselves in self-begotten suits of armor, and now as if in solidarity against the coming storm, they pointed their wide-angled beaks at the opaque stew of roiling clouds.

While the rattle and scream of trucks and cars hurtled back-and-forth on the highway, Matt and I joined this tripod army, peering through our cameras, and panned around at the breadth and grandeur of this storm. The storm's anvil extended like an endless pancake far above to the east, and an advancing line of lower smaller cumuliform clouds drifted overhead—heralds of the more powerful flank of the storm where we could see the ragged wall cloud, sugar-white hail core, and glittering pulses of lightning. Thin rusty films appeared to extend from the storm base towards the ground: possibly rain curtains that might indicate tornadic circulation. Yet, once again, the storm was passing on with no clear demonstration of visible rotation.

A more promising storm lurked behind this one, and it was time to go south on Highway 6 to get a look. This third storm of our day had already overshadowed the sky with its bulk, so we could see no anvil, but were submerged beneath charcoal rolls of ominous stratus. Once again, we pulled over when we spotted the lowered slant of a wall cloud. This time the wall cloud was far closer to our location than with the previous storms, and not only did the radar indicate a hook forming but we saw some upward motion of scud clouds rising in curls towards the base of the storm. No funnel, but this storm was actively developing. Frighteningly close lightning stabbed the ground. We retreated from the ripping thunder and too-close-for-comfort proximity of the wall cloud—driving farther south on 6.

This is where we made our logistical mistake. Technically, we should have tried to stay ahead of the storm by going north on 6, perhaps east then on 287 and tried to enter the network of primitive roads closer to the Red River. But we were afraid of getting trapped between an imminent tornado and the river, without access to a crossing. Or getting stuck in the mud once the deluge unleashed itself and sloppy brown glop clenched around the tires, ending our progress while baseball-sized hail might bash the glass of the windows. Indeed, we could see a thick curtain of white to the left of the wall cloud; one would have thought of a white-out blizzard enveloping a mountain slope in the Rockies, not a Spring day in Texas. We didn't want to drive north and risk getting into that hail, or being right beneath the wall cloud, which had taken on a more aggressive appearance, collared and darker, angling ever more sharply and lower. It loomed over a farmhouse to the North, a tapioca cluster of aerie density.

Aside from wanting to avoid those perils of hail-thrashing, flood-flashing, and mud-mucking paralysis, we saw before us still approaching a striking clear slot—where no precipitation appeared to be falling, and the invisible rear flank downdraft wind had scoured out an arc in the clouds.

Then, amid this calm and sunny white space, we could see distinct rotation.

It came slowly, and you had to steady your gaze to perceive it, but it was undeniable. Furthermore, not more than perhaps a couple-hundred feet above the field we could see silver-grey wisps of cloud forming and rising. We believed we were witnessing the birth of a second area of storm rotation: a new wall cloud that might soon form a funnel and tornado before our very eyes. However, technically we were rather too close to the cooler downdraft sculpted gust front of the hook of the storm to expect a tornadic epiphany, especially when the shelf cloud of the hook arced behind the clear-slot, signaling the end of warm moist air that fed the updraft. Yet, how convenient to stay where we were and hope that from that dazzling indigo-sculpted washboard underbelly of cloud a rain-free twister might snake down and dance in that field.

Meanwhile the storm was officially tornado-warned, and Matt and I debated whether this were merely because of radar indications or back to the north where the lightning-wreathed wall cloud had drifted on with its curtains of hail, a tornado had in fact been spotted, wrapped in cloaks of ice, rain, and debris. We would later learn that a tornado indeed had begun which crossed the Red River while baseball-sized hail shattered windshields and dented roofs.

But before our own eyes, we witnessed a curling of clouds at the edge of the clear slot, accompanied by a slight lowering. Our fabled second wall cloud appeared to be emerging, yet it did no more than tease with curlicues while beneath that wall of hail to our north the real titan raged, unknown to us. Yet, spellbound, we had plenty to see as the clouds circled counter-clockwise, a dark carousel between us and the ivory glint of sunlight in the clear slot beyond.

The storm moved on, and while we watched the larger view, we noticed our new wall cloud never dipped as low as the one earlier—buried in blankets of hail where what would be called the Elmer tornado whirled in a frenzy of clay, hay, mud, insulation, dirt, and dust.

We witnessed other storms, and certainly there were beautiful iridescent sculptures of water and ice that drifted over those Spring-green fields. We saw more striated anvils, knobby with mammatus nodes, grainy-topped cauliflower clouds whose summits bulged like brain corral, implying meteorological malice as they directed the tumult of hail and wind.

Because cell networks kept failing among our travels past stormy ranchland, we turned to the weather radio, but so much severe weather had spread across the southern plains that the pandemonic whining of alerts did little to guide us. At some point, jostling my laptop, as I struggled to reload the latest radar image that would indicate our vehicle's position relative to the storms, I inadvertently snapped the weather radio's antennae. Chaos always joins the chase.

On our way back to Wichita Falls, we stopped again at the McDonald's and marveled over photographs and film footage shared with us by other chasers—all of whom admitted to their cracked windshields and dinged side-mirrors, a price they seemed more than willing to have paid. None whom we met that saw the tornado had escaped unscathed, at least as far as their vehicles went. But they had the pride of interception. No one was hurt to our knowledge. Unlike the fate of my father's cousin, who in 1974 was pulled from her mobile home in Belleville, Ohio, clutching her baby. Mother and daughter both survived, but that cousin is paralyzed for life. Yet, she has lived fully, so "paralysis" always seems like something of an unjust term, though it fits the fate of her lower extremities. Storms change lives.

I remember the flash and rumble of thunder in Sacramento. When I was three-years-old, I dragged a cardboard box out onto the covered patio, and I thrilled to the staccato drumming of rain and some pea-sized hail chattering in bursts above me. I felt secure and yet wildly excited to be part of the storm. Known for its mild weather—aside from those endless one-hundred-degree days of summer—California still opened the storm window for me. I crawled right through. Living in

Texas, there's a wind blowing towards me and towards which I must continually move.

Envy and guilt also drift with these storms. How can one ever feel free to celebrate the evolutionary potential of a meteorological nature if that atmospheric climax involves potential destruction and loss of life? How can one believe an unimpeded view of a tornado is ever earned and that it's not just a matter of getting off lucky—this time—when so many others have endured property damage, injury, and even faced death? If Matt and I had set aside our reservations about safety, and picked the right turns on the right roads, we might too have seen the threads of cloud that descended from our storm that twisted north of Odell, Texas, and southwest of Elmer, Oklahoma, and coiled into a dusty violent wedge that thundered across the Red River.

No reason to lament what might have been—not when each year titanic clouds rise above the Lone Star State. It's well known that Texas reports the most tornadoes, and that's for a good reason. There's plenty of room here to take advantage of the heat, moisture, and shear, as winds plummet over the Rockies and plow north from the Gulf, flooding Houston, deluging hill country, and breeding monsters in the Texas panhandle. The smallest cottonball of cloud has its chance to supernova into a god of the skies, to reach out from on high to drag through the dust a corona of earth and air, a wind that scours the land and trembles through the soul.

Let me tell you something else we saw as we waited out another storm before leaving the McDonald's for the second time that day. Most of the supercells had passed, and what chasers call a storm of a more "linear" fashion approached Vernon, bringing a torrent of rain and such high winds that when I curiously opened the door, the gust snatched the door from my grasp and hurled it against the outside glass. Luckily, nothing broke, and I was able to reclose the door by tugging hard with both hands. And everyone in the restaurant watched with a certain awe as the maelstrom raged outside.

Except for one family. A couple with their young children—elementary-school ages—perhaps seven and nine—headed out the same door that got whipped away from me by the wind. The father opened the door with a scowl on his bearded face, and the mother came too—with a sullen but equally hard-headed expression. The two children, looking scared but resigned, followed in their wake. Perhaps the parents had a notion there was no tornado lurking in that storm—or they simply didn't care. They had things to do. Places to go. The weather was something to endure, but not mighty enough an impediment that day to ultimately stand in those Texans' way.

Not that a reaction of indifference or annoyance to the storms always divides longterm-Texans from recent arrivals. Consider this: when Matt and I left Wichita Falls later that evening, as the sun was setting, yet another supercell came from the southwest. This supercell was the prototypical "mothership," was tornado-warned on radar, and with its upside-down layer-cake mesocyclone, there was a look of such well-inscribed fearful symmetry that it was hard to believe a tornado wouldn't emerge, flinging cars and cows about mercilessly in the wet and dark.

We'd stopped at a gas station, and as we finished our transactions, a gust of wind rushed out from this coming storm. Trash and dust whirled across the parking lot. Grit hit the gas station windows and rattled the roof. Everyone hurried to their vehicles. Some pick-up truck roared off as though pursued by the Devil. We too went on our way, blasting too fast through a clatter of rain. If a tornado were on its way, we wanted to be well ahead of it. There was no point searching for the dark sublime in that night as that mothership made her sinister landing.

All the other Texans seemed in agreement that storm was nothing to mess around with. Native or tourist, that gas station became empty of folks so fast it would make your head spin.

Even if nothing twirled in the night while cars raced with rain and wind, we'd had several memorable turns in the rotations of Texas weather. We'd seen something of the indomitable passions and fierce determinations that drive people to make their way through these titanic phantoms of storm. We'd reached through the vapor and wind and felt other hands, lined with grime of muddy roads, and lives led close to the pulse of lightning, the groan of car engines, the patter of rain. It's hard labor— revolving our world till we face another grinding blast of wind.

Come Again Another Day
William Jensen

His name was Travis, and he needed to steal a car. Everyone on the radio said the storm was going to be bad, and he wanted to get out of town before it hit. He'd already slid past the sedans and station wagons at the motel and peeked through their windows for unlocked doors. Now Travis prowled the H.E.B. parking lot hoping to find some Ford or Chevrolet. He kept his head down as he moved. Women with big hair pushed their carts out of the store. The wheels of the carts rattled on the pavement. It was only a quarter past five but the sky already looked stained with coal. He figured he had half an hour.

Travis was nineteen and had previously spent an eight-month stint at the Buck County Correctional Ranch, but he faced serious time if he stuck around Santa Clara, Texas. Last night he ran away with his girlfriend who happened to be the mayor's sixteen-year-old daughter.

Laura Dell waited for him at the Lone Star Lodge. He'd left her sitting on the bed in her underwear with a stash of candy: Pixy Stix, Smarties, Lemonheads. Travis didn't know how she lived off a diet that was almost all sugar. He wasn't sure if he'd ever seen her eat anything that wasn't sweet, but he promised himself he'd buy her all the Jujubes and Gummy Bears she could stand if they escaped Santa Clara.

He found an old pick-up with a rolled down window at the back of the lot. He didn't see any keys in the ignition, but he knew how to hotwire it and figured some cowboy's truck wouldn't draw much attention. He looked over his shoulder and got in. He hadn't fiddled with a car's wires in a while, but he stripped and weaved them and got the engine to turn just as the storm's first drops fell on the windshield.

Driving through town, Travis gnawed on his lip and listened to Marty Robins on the AM. He understood it would be easier to go on without Laura Dell but that wasn't an option. It had been her idea to run away, so he was sure she wanted the same things as him, and he wanted many things: a decent job, a nice home, maybe even a health club membership where he and Laura Dell could play tennis (he didn't know the game but he could learn). He tightened his grip on the steering wheel. All they had to do was drive, he told himself. It was just that easy.

The rain got stronger, so he flipped on the lights and wipers, and by the time he pulled up to the Lone Star Lodge, torrents thick as quilts came sideways in the wind. He put the truck in park but left it running while he sprinted to the room and knocked on the door. Laura Dell was still in her bra and panties when she answered. Travis saw the pile of candy wrappers on the floor. All of their clothes lay on the bed.

"Didn't you pack?"

"You didn't say anything about packing. You just said I was to wait here."

"I got us a car, but the storm is going to be bad. We've got to move before they close the roads."

"I don't know why you're in such a rush. Is it Daddy? I bet he doesn't even know I'm gone."

"Oh, I've got a feeling he does, sweet-pea. I'd bet all the oil at Spindletop. Now get your pants on."

Travis stuffed the shirts and socks into their suitcases as fast as he could. Laura Dell pulled on her jeans and picked at her blouses. Her amber hair swayed as she moved. Travis watched her but didn't say anything. She was short and skinny and spoke like a chipmunk except for when she was hungry, then she sounded like Rottweiler. Laura Dell slipped on a violet tunic and began modeling in front of the mirror.

"Do you like this? I'm not sure if the color works."

"It's fine," said Travis. He ran the suitcases out to the truck, his boots splashing in dirty puddles. He saw a bolt of lightning, bright as hot piss, zigzag down in the distance. It made him gasp and pause. He rushed back to the room. Laura Dell now wore a pink tank-top in front of the mirror. She started to say something but Travis didn't let her finish.

"We don't have time for this. This storm is going to make Noah look like a baby crying in the shallow end of the pool. If the police find us, you know what will happen? I'll go to jail. And jail isn't wacky happy fun time. It's jail."

"I'm just trying on a few outfits. Let me take a shower and we can leave."

Travis stood there, dripping wet, and looked at Laura Dell. He felt something inside him tighten like a fist. If he took off now, without her, he could get out of town and not have to worry about cops or jail, but he clenched his jaw and forced those thoughts out of his mind. He wanted to start shouting at her. But he didn't. He wanted to scream at her. But he didn't. She posed in front of the mirror. He heard the rain sloshing down outside, and he heard cars rushing over the wet streets toward some place safe and dry. He didn't say anything. He went to Laura Dell and grabbed her. She yelped and kicked. She had a lot of fight in her considering how small she was. Travis threw her over his shoulder as he imagined a barbarian would, and she punched his shoulders and back. He carried her to the truck and shoved her into the cab. She scooted on the bench seat away from him. Wet hair fell over her eyes. She cursed him, but Travis couldn't hear her over the downpour. He got the last few items from the room and then got in the truck with Laura Dell.

"You're an animal," she said.

"King of the jungle, baby."

Laura Dell wouldn't speak to him as they rode through town. Weather advisory announcements screeched over the radio. Travis steered past the courthouse, the Dairy Queen, and the Whataburger and made his way to the outskirts of Santa Clara where the ranchers and the farmers worked and lived. The windshield wipers couldn't keep up with the rain. He had to drive slowly just to see where he was going. A few cop cars rushed by with their lights and sirens on, but they were heading elsewhere. The emergency sirens started blaring just as Travis turned onto the highway.

Their plan had been to go to California and live on the beach, but as they cruised into the West, Travis felt an uneasy weight press down on him. He told himself he could relax once they made it to New Mexico. Then they could celebrate and really begin a life. Travis looked at Laura Dell and tried to give her a reassuring smile. She leaned her body against the door and wouldn't look at him. He drove on.

At one point he reached across the bench seat and put a hand on Laura Dell's forearm. He left it there. She looked at him but said nothing. They drove slowly through the storm. He muttered something to her about how everything was going to be okay, but even he wasn't sure of how true that was. He knew he didn't sound convincing.

"You're awfully quiet," he said.

"Can't believe you picked me up like that. I'm not just luggage, you know. I'm a person."

Travis bit his lip and kept driving. He recognized the dangers of running away with Laura Dell. If he was caught with an underage girl, they'd really lock him up. But he didn't think he could stay away from her. Her body always felt hot and raw when he held her. On those nights when they took off their clothes and kissed in the dark, she tasted of wildflowers and honey. Whenever she was close to him, he felt calm, and he wanted to spend everyday with his head on her chest, her warm skin, so he could listen to her heart beat.

He pulled off the highway and onto a thin and empty ranch road that ran deeper into the storm. Lightning bolts flashed as twisted, fighting snakes and disappeared. Travis used both hands on the steering wheel, and after a few miles he turned onto a stretch of dirt and gravel that usually looked beige and tan in the sun but now appeared dark as rust with the rain.

"Is this safe?" said Laura Dell.

"Too many cops on the highway. Got to stick to the back roads. This will cut across the county. It'll be dirty, but we'll get there."

"That doesn't answer my question."

Travis drove slowly and prayed not to get stuck in the mud. The road curved and sloped into an arroyo that was flooded with copper-colored rapids. Logs and branches and debris floated in the stream, and currents slapped over boulders and stumps that sat in the bed of the arroyo. Water rushed down the side of the cliff and under the truck.

"I think you should turn back," said Laura Dell.

"Can't do it."

"I don't feel safe. I don't want to do this."

"Don't want to do what? I can handle it. I know what I'm doing."

"You couldn't even handle working in the courthouse mailroom. Are you illiterate? No wonder you got sent to the ranch. So stupid you got caught making yourself a grilled cheese."

Travis felt that tight-fist feeling again, and it grew bigger this time. It was almost as if it took up all of his insides. He started to grind his teeth. He wasn't sure how long he could keep that feeling from bursting into something loud and stupid that he would regret.

"I'm trying to focus here."

"I bet you got that early release because you weren't smart enough to get any work done out there."

"You want to bitch at me, fine. Just do it later."

"I thought you were some big rebel. You're just a big old—"

Laura Dell never finished her sentence. A wave of rain and mud and gunk hit them and rocked the pick-up to the side. Before Travis could take a deep breath, before sense could be made or an escape could be planned, the truck's wheels slid down the slope and the vehicle crashed into the river. The impact sounded like an explosion. Travis and Laura Dell ricocheted off the doors, and water began to seep in and fill the cab.

The water kept coming. Laura Dell shrieked. She had a cut on her forehead, and a trail of blood ran over her left eyebrow. She held up her hands as if being mugged.

The water rose to their knees. It was so cold it felt as if someone had inserted frozen slabs of metal under the skin around the calves and shins. Travis unbuckled Laura Dell's seatbelt and then his own. He leaned back on the bench seat and kicked out the driver's side window. The glass shattered in large shards and wedges, and the rest of the floodwaters gushed into the pick-up, and with the water came the stink of the soil, garbage, and the scum off the bottoms of stones. Travis took Laura Dell by the wrist and began to half-crawl and half-swim out the window and into the swift current. He held onto her as firmly as he could. Laura Dell yelped. There was only the cold, wet roar of the river and the rain. Travis was swept under and away and lost his grip of Laura Dell. Clumsily, he slapped the stream trying to find her. He kicked at the ground with his toes but could never stand or stay in one place. The rapids shoved him onward and pushed him below the surface so he had to fight to raise his head and inhale as much air as he could before it all started again. He couldn't see Laura Dell. He couldn't see the truck. The world was nothing but brown and silver blurs filled with random items and trash rushing by and occasionally colliding with one another then drifting on again.

He flailed at branches that swept past him. He grabbed at everything until he bashed into a large rock. At first his ribs and knees hurt, but then came the relief of not fighting the river. He laid his head on top of the rock and closed his eyes and breathed. He just let his lungs send sweet, wonderful oxygen into his body. He heard the rain hitting the water, the river rushing around him, and the wind bellowing through the rain. The water no longer felt cold, it was only wet and thick and heavy. His hands had turned pale and clammy, and his fingers didn't seem to work well. They twitched and felt fragile as twigs. He kept his cheek on the rock and breathed through his mouth.

Mud slid off the bank in chunks as the river rose and grew. Plastic bags and an old door floated by. He didn't know what happened to Laura Dell. His teeth chattered so hard he thought he'd break a molar. He tried saying her name, but his voice vanished with the howl of the wind.

He rested and gathered his strength. He was close to the bank and knew if he didn't shove off the boulder soon the flood would eventually grow and swallow him. After taking several deep breaths, after cursing himself and the whole rotten town of Santa Clara, he clenched his jaw and threw his body to the right as far and hard as he could. He splashed and disappeared beneath the water. When his head broke the surface, gasping for air, he realized he could touch the bottom of the river. The current pushed at him so he had to crawl and paw his way through the gunk and the dredge. He dragged himself onto the loose, moist earth and collapsed. His right hand clenched the dirt. He fell asleep with a fistful of sludge.

When he awoke, he found that not only had the stormed passed but that the sun was out and hot and bright. Mud had dried and caked his jeans, boots, and the front of his shirt. It even matted his hair. Travis stood and looked about. The river was still strong and fast though not nearly as violent as it had been. He didn't see Laura Dell anywhere.

He marched upstream and called her name. He looked for her body among the fords and bars. He tried not to think. Some things were never helped by thinking. He believed all he needed to do was move and pay attention. The rest was beyond his control.

He walked on for almost an hour. His boots stuck in the mud and made sucking sounds when he pulled up his feet. The sun burned the back of his neck and the tops of his ears. He could even feel the heat on his scalp beneath his hair. His mouth turned dry, his lips chapped. He shouted Laura Dell's name until his throat ached.

He found her sprawled in the weeds near a grove of cottonwoods. She didn't move. She was barefoot and her blouse was ripped along the back. He kneeled by her body and put two fingers on her neck to see if there was a pulse. Her skin felt warm. She opened her eyes, looked at him, and looked away almost as if ashamed.

"I want to go home," she said.

Travis nodded.

"That sounds like a good idea."

He helped her up and made sure she was okay. No major cuts. No broken bones. And then they walked away from the river and up the walls of the arroyo beneath the splintering sun. The land looked baked and warped, and all of the bushes were bent and smashed. The couple trekked on and after a while they held hands, but he knew it was not romantic. Eventually, they came to a paved road covered with dust and mud. Weeds had washed up and snagged in the barbed wire beside the road. Travis and Laura Dell looked to their left and their right. The sun felt hot and gross.

Travis saw a truck coming their way. He stepped onto the pavement and began waving his arms. Laura Dell squatted and picked pebbles and dirt from the bottom of her feet. The truck stopped, and the driver rolled down his window. He was an old cowboy with a white moustache.

"You two look like you need a vacation."

"We got caught in the storm," said Travis.

"Get in, I'll take you to town."

Travis glanced over his shoulder at Laura Dell. That tight-fist feeling in his chest wasn't there anymore. He didn't feel anything now when he looked at her. He waited for her to say something, but she said nothing. She just sat there and stared at him in a way that made her seem much older than sixteen.

"Actually," said Travis. "Just take her. She's got people worried about her."

"You sure?"

"I've got elsewhere to be."

Travis helped Laura Dell into the cowboy's truck. After she buckled up, she looked at Travis and shook her head.

"Goodbye, Ms. Beam."

"Goodbye, Mr. Bondurant."

Travis shut her door. He waved as the truck drove away and shrank along the blacktop. Eventually he couldn't even see it. Travis stared at his hands caked with mud, almost like gloves. He turned and began walking in the opposite direction, sticking out his thumb in hopes of hitching a ride.

The Weather and Texas Pride
Dave Kuhne

As the chunks of ice fell from the sky, I opened the passenger door to my pickup and waved the woman and child into the cab.

"Come on. *Pase.*"

I had seen the woman and the little girl waiting for the bus when I pulled into the bay only fifteen minutes earlier. They climbed into the truck.

The ice beat down, denting the roof of the bay. One baseball-size hailstone bounced off the hood of my pickup, leaving a scar. Cars pulled onto the lot, crowding into the shelter of the bays, and the hail began to whiten the street. On Cleburne Road, a truck jumped the curb, its windshield shattered by the stones of ice. The woman and I didn't bother to talk; the pounding of the hail on the roof of the bay made talking impossible. The little girl put her hands over her ears. For five minutes the ice crashed down like shrapnel.

The only people who pay more attention to the weather than the owners of car washes are the on-air professionals. In fact, I had been watching the weather closely all afternoon as the sky darkened and the bright red bands inched from west to east across the TV radar. I had decided to make a last minute check on the location, but the storm moved in faster than I expected.

My uncle Jake, who owned the Texas Pride self-serve car wash before me, had even included a special section on weather in the owner's manual he left me, a booklet titled *Maintaining Texas Pride*. Most of the weather entries had to do with some event that affected the car wash income: dust and mud storms that left every car in town splattered with a patina of dirt, and ice storms, which guaranteed at least two weeks of good business as customers tried to get the salt and grime off their cars. And there were always the floods, the droughts, the deep freezes, and the extended periods of heat.

The ice finally stopped falling and the temperature dropped. Green-tinged clouds raced from west to east in the wake of the storm.

"*Gracias,*" the woman said.

She smiled and helped her daughter down from the cab. They began walking, slowly because of the hail, north on Cleburne Road, past the bus stop and across the street to *Las Ramblas*, the drive-through beer joint staffed by bikini-clad girls on roller skates.

I did a quick walk around the lot, looking for damage. The roofs over both the wet and dry bays were heavily dented by the hail, as was the warp-around facade on the wet bay roof, but that damage was only cosmetic. The cars on the lot didn't fare so well. Most of them had at least one window or windshield shattered by the ice. So far as I could tell, no one was hurt.

Once the hail melted off the streets, business began to boom, not with people washing their cars, but with people vacuuming the broken windshield glass from the car interiors. Seeing the cars begin to line up at each of my vacs, I headed back to the home office for my collection buckets and the tools I'd need to clean the vac traps. Cleaning vac traps was a job I usually farmed out to Big John, the neighborhood idiot savant and former grad student at TCU (a philosophy major) who often found "treasures" in the traps. But the boom in business demanded that I do the dirty work myself.

Driving through the neighborhood, I could see that the damage was widespread: cars and houses with broken windows, a roof blown half off of a convenience store, tree branches down on the streets. It was a miracle that the power was still on. Without power, I would have to stay at the lot and wave away potential customers. I was amazed that people would get angry at *me* because the power was out, as if *I* would kill the power to my own business just to get *them* riled up, to delay their pressing need to hose down some old junker. One thing I had learned since I inherited Texas Pride from my uncle was that the public had very little, especially limits on behavior, and knew next to nothing. But some people call me an elite academic snob.

Jake's house in South Hills was perfectly designed for running a coin-op car wash so I moved in when I inherited the place. There was an alarm system, several surveillance cameras that eyed the front and back yards, and bars that protected the doors and windows. Following Jake's example, I kept a pistol in every room and a shotgun behind the "office" door. I checked for storm damage. The burglar bars had protected the windows, but the house would need a new roof. Probably every house in Tarrant County would need a new roof. I got my collection keys and buckets as well some leather gloves and a small shovel and drove back to Texas Pride.

The wash bays were empty, but the lines of cars at the vacuums snaked off the lot and onto the adjacent streets. In some neighborhoods, that might have been a problem, but not off Cleburne Road. The area had become a sort of anything goes no man's land where the cops and local business owners stood off the invasion of newcomers and gang members who seemed to be forever cruising. And then there was the endless parade of drug addicts, drunks, and prostitutes who trolled the car wash looking for dope, spare change, or customers.

I spent the afternoon emptying out the vac bins (if they were full of windshield glass, the vacs would have no suction) and collecting the money from each of the eight vac safes. I was charging fifty cents for a three minute vac, and the safes could each hold about three hundred dollars in quarters. As usual, I carried my .32 auto in my pocket and my .38 in a waistband holster. In spite of the heavy use, the vacs held up well; I only had to replace one burnt out motor. I emptied the safes every couple of hours; it was going to be a record day for the vacs, which, next to the vending machines that dispensed air freshener, towels, and condoms, were the highest profit machines on the lot. As I loaded the buckets of quarters into my truck, it occurred to me that even hailstorms can have a silver lining.

The hailstorm made me recall some of the other weather events Jake, my late uncle, had recorded in the *Maintaining Texas Pride* journal. Of course, Jake was a native Texan, and Texans had a sense of pride about everything associated with their state, including the weather. When it came to weather, Texas was a land of epic hurricanes, tornadoes, and floods; a place where droughts lasted years, heat waves melted the highways, and sudden deep freezes shattered plants, animals, people, and equipment. Yet even when Fort Worth was silenced by white cold, the grapefruit grew in the Valley and bikini-clad college girls walked the beach at South Padre.

As the new owner of Texas Pride Car Wash, I found that my exposure to weather was greater than I had expected. Naturally, I had seen some weather when I had taught at South West Panhandle State in Brownfield, but I spent most of those Panhandle winters reading post-apocalyptic fiction and "tutoring" my favorite grad student, Pam, who later took a job as a teacher in Throckmorton. In the summers I headed for the Colorado Rockies where you didn't even need AC. Besides, all my classes were in a modern, red brick building that was overheated in the winter and frosty cold in the summer, so once I made my way to campus from my doublewide on the edge of town, I was pretty much sheltered. But at Texas Pride, the weather could not be avoided or ignored. Working the Texas Pride Car Wash was a clear example of Naturalism: nature was completely indifferent to man or machine.

Jake had noted in *Maintaining Texas Pride* that ice storms were the most serious of the weather threats, at least from a car washing point of view. Sure, there would be dirty cars lined up at the wash bays for two weeks after a good ice storm, but before you could wash cars you had to have power, and ice storms could easily knock the power out for days. To keep the equipment from freezing if an ice storm did knock out the electricity, Jake had installed a gas space heater that would insure the temperature in the room would stay at least forty, protecting the pumps and storage vats from cracking.

After I stacked the buckets of quarters (six buckets at about $500 a bucket meant at least $3,000—a new one day vac record) in the counting room and popped open a beer, I glanced though Jake's chapter on weather. The *Maintaining Texas Pride* booklet was really just a hundred lined pages in a loose-leaf binder, the pages filled with Jake's clean scrawl, comma splices and all.

The chapter on the weather was one of the longest ones and was arranged in chronological order. The first entries described the New Year's Eve ice storm of 1978, a storm that shut down Dallas and Fort Worth for days. It was the first year that Jake owned Texas Pride, and he wrote that because of the ice he "couldn't drive the streets so I walked three miles each way to check the location. Just about froze my ass. Power was out but the space heater was holding the equipment room to 47 degrees. Weep system to each of the wet bays was working, keeping the water lines from freezing." And then, several days later: "After the thaw business boomed. Had to rob the safes each day cause they were filling up."

Business wasn't so good during the legendary heat wave of the summer of 1980. Jake wrote that "it's been over a hundred with no rain for more than forty days, hit 112 twice, and the temperature in the equipment room topped 130. When I come by, twice a day, I make sure I leave a large ice chest filled with bottled water by the equipment room door. Also leave a bowl of water for dogs. This way, the homeless and the prostitutes (and anyone else) can get water without fooling with the outside sink. Been doing this for two weeks, and no one's stolen the ice chest yet. I'm surprised."

In the two semesters (spring and fall—yes, I still measured time in academic terms) that I had owned the car wash, I had been surprised by the weather several times. Twice, I had been forced to take cover in the equipment room when the tornado sirens sounded, and once I had narrowly avoided spinning off Cleburne Road during a thunderstorm that flooded the street. But even more surprising than the weather were the people and their relationships to their cars despite the weather. One hundred and fifteen heat index? No problem! I'm waxing the sports car. Cold rain falling? Won't stop me from using the tire cleaner! Five above zero and a twenty mile per hour north wind? Damn water freezes on impact but I'm soaping this sucker down for the holidays!

I ignored these folks and came to the obvious conclusion that people love their cars. Lots of important life events happen in cars; I'd seen several myself since taking over Texas Pride. Sometimes the only relationship people had was with their vehicles. And the way things had been going, more than a few people had resorted to calling their cars home.

The last entry Jake had made about the weather had been almost a year earlier, right before he died and I quit my position at Southwest Panhandle State to take over the Texas Pride Wash. It was hard to believe that a year had passed so fast. I vaguely remembered the storm that Jake wrote about. It was a mud-dust storm that hit Brownfield, where the college is, just hours before blowing into Ft. Worth. This was a rare weather event that combined elements of a dust storm with a thunderstorm. The rains fell through the blowing dust, forming blobs of brown mud that splattered all the cars to Jake's great delight.

In the other room the television blared a bleak teaser: "Dozens injured in Mayfest hail storm, details at ten."

I picked up a pen and made an entry in the Texas Pride weather log, starting where Uncle Jake had left off and trying to echo his prose style: "Early May hail storm blows out windshields, damages buildings, injures dozens at Mayfest. Record one day vac take due to the broken windshield glass."

I had made my first contribution to *Maintaining Texas Pride*. I took a long drink of beer and toasted Uncle Jake and Texas weather.

Airborne
Paula Starche

Roy turned thirteen and I turned eleven the year the floods came. In addition to managing the ranch, Dad had to add a second job working for the oil company, checking pumps and registering the production levels.

The land was parched, and black tabosa grass clung to the dirt where it could. With biblical drama, it had not rained in seven years. Elmer Kelton wrote a book about this named *The Time It Never Rained*. Big dust storms blew in from the northwest making the sky brown and leaving sand on the inside window sills and in our throats. The cowboys on the ranch covered their mouths with their bandannas.

Inside, Roy and I and our four younger brothers watched John Wayne stand off all the rustlers. The house nestled at the base of Monument Hill, so named for an Indian mound at its top. Snakes, rabies, and scorpions were our natural enemies, but the odds were with us and we prevailed. After all we had our father, good with a shotgun and a shovel and not afraid. One evening we had a rabid fox at the back door. "Bring me the gun, Frankie," yelled Dad, and I ran like the wind. At night he fortified himself with Pearl beer.

I haven't said anything about our mother. She was a nervous type, but she was right there, cooking, changing a diaper, and if possible, reading a book. In the morning she made me stay still while she braided my auburn hair. Afterwards I helped her wash the cloth diapers and hang them in the yard.

"Frankie, put your fingers between the soft skin and the diaper," she said, showing me how to guide the safety pin through the tough cloth without puncturing the baby.

She taught me how to pour the condensed milk into the sterilized bottles and feed the baby in the early morning. In the evenings Mom would read to us and tell stories of growing up in Chicago, a place with movie theaters and candy stores. At night she fingered her silver beaded rosary as she went to sleep.

As soon as we were seven or eight and could sit on a horse, we would ride with Dad and the other cowboys to help with the round ups. The orange pink sun announced the day's arrival as the horses were saddled. It was a source of pride to have legs long enough to swing up into the saddle without a helping hand from one of the men. That was the year the stirrups were lowered on my saddle and I moved up to a bigger horse named Pepper.

Some mornings we rode over the railroad tracks to the middle pasture. On windy days tumbleweeds, just as in the movies, would sweep across the roads and pasture. My brothers and I could contain the sheep once the cowboys had them gathered. When we rode back we held tightly to the reins to keep the horses from bolting for the barn. Otherwise we would be on a runaway and likely thrown.

In the evenings we heard our parents talking about the drought and fretting about how to find money for school clothes. My father thought Mom spent too much money so we felt guilty about the things we had. We kept quiet about shoes that pinched or flapped. If only it would rain, we knew we would be all right. It was affording the feed for the cattle that was worrying Dad and causing their arguments at night.

There was a dry creek bed a hundred yards in front of the ranch house. A great blue heron came through that spring and stood majestically in the draw. An omen of promise. The bird possessed the draw even more than the red-tailed hawks that flew overhead. One weekend our uncle brought his small plane out to the ranch. "Who wants to go up for a ride?" he asked. He brought a kite with him and it seemed to rise up into the clouds. I confused the two events and believed I had traveled up to the top of the kite.

One week in early October, the rain began. We ran out doors in our bare feet, chilly, but energized by the water dripping down our faces, licking the drops. Roy found the slippery baby frogs first. He handed one to me in his cupped hands as a present. I made a soft cave for it with my palms and felt the tickle of its little feet. My mother was behind us holding my youngest brother in her arms. All of us were drenched and yelping with joy. When my father arrived in his truck, we went inside, leaving the doors and windows open for the evening. I kept the little frog in a jar by my bed and let it go the next morning.

Our good mood lasted through the next day, even better because Dad had to stay home from work. When he went out to check the draw, he found the water level too high to cross in his pick-up. Not even the school bus could cross. It was a perfect day for hopping in puddles and counting baby frogs. Drowned ants floated by in little rivulets. We had never even seen an umbrella. Dust in and out of the house was replaced with mud. Sam and Joe wrestled with each other in the living room until Dad shouted at them to "Quit that noise!" and raised a ruckus himself. Later the second youngest, John, slipped out the door in his diaper and was up at the corral before anyone noticed. That evening the phone line went down in the rain.

We heard the rain through the night and our hopes were high. There would be grass for the livestock and continued ranch work for Dad. We would run barefoot in the cool grass of the yard.

The next morning I curled up with Sam to read *Charlotte's Web* aloud. I felt an urge to look out the front door. Dirty brown water swirled up against the bottom edge of the door sill. We were flooded and we were marooned. Dad and Mom gathered up the youngest in their arms and we waded the fifty yards to the corral. Turning right out the back gate, we climbed up the path to the hill. Once we were on higher ground, Dad and Roy went back for the station wagon and truck and drove them up on the hill. The two of them went back down to save as much of our clothing and furniture as possible. The rest of us watched their movements from the car.

Roy was tall for his age and very strong, but the water was rising so Dad put him on the most solid horse, Blucher. Dad stayed afoot. Mom was worried and wanted them to come back up, but I felt sure they could manage. I felt guilty for not being with them. Dad said I was the best of us all on horseback and I could be helping. I was wondering how the sheep were fairing when I noticed that Roy had headed Blucher down in the direction of the draw. What on earth was he doing? I could see that Dad was yelling at him, but Roy couldn't hear. Then I saw his objective. A lamb had become tangled in the mesquite and bee brush along the road and he had set out to free it before it drowned.

As he reached the lamb and leaned down out of his saddle to pull at the branches, Blucher panicked and tossed Roy into the water. He reached for a thick branch but the water whirled around him and sucked him down toward the rising creek. Our father grabbed a long rope from the fencepost of the corral and waded desperately in Roy's direction. He reached the horse and swung on to the saddle. We lost sight of all three of them within a few minutes.

This was the first but not the last time in my life that my mind expressed no thought at all in a crisis. Although everyone in the car was crying or yelling I had a sense of complete silence. Both the worst and nothing at all had happened. It was Sam who shook me, "There's a radio in the truck, Frankie!"

Our closest neighbor was three miles away with a muddy back road for access, but we could try. Sam had played with the radio behind Dad's back so knew how to work it. Our neighbor answered that he was

84

headed our way and would leave his wife at their house to call to the nearest town for help.

It was about noon when our neighbor and Dad walked up the hill without Roy. A quick call to our neighbor's wife gave us little information, but she had spoken with the sheriff in our nearby town. We had no food or water so the neighbor went back for his wagon and some supplies. As he left, his wife's voice came over the radio. There was a chance that a helicopter enroute back to the Goodfellow Air Force Base could look for Roy. It was getting later in the day, but it was less than an hour away.

We heard it before we saw it, of course. The rotors made the same noise as on *Whirlybirds* but I did not feel the confidence I had in the TV heroes. Dad waved them in the suspected direction of Roy from the ground while our neighbor tried to maintain radio contact. The flow of the water would have been obvious from the air and the helicopter began moving back and forth as it went down Spring Creek. It disappeared from sight. Our neighbor had brought provisions so we children could eat. The grownups had no interest in food.

About 4:00 as the late afternoon light began to change, we were radioed that Roy had been sighted. He was high in an oak near the fence line at the road. He had been swept into a whirling area which broke the water's force just enough for him to climb up into the tree's branches. Thirty or so minutes later we received the news that they had successfully lowered and raised their rescue ropes and he was in the helicopter. It was not safe to land and they were taking him to Goodfellow. They passed back over us as they left the ranch. There were tears all around. "I wish I had a Pearl," said Dad, but it was long gone.

The ground was impassable for a car, but we had enough light to make it to the neighbor's house by horse drawn wagon. The next morning we learned the flood waters had peaked at four feet in our house.

That was our first flood. The next one was in April, and the third was the following September. Neither of these reached the house. Dad was able to quit his second job, and we had an extra cow hand graduated from short pants to ride on the round ups.

By then my legs were long and the grass was tall, waving to the blue, cloudless sky.

Birds of the Storm God
Jeffrey DeLotto

The old Tejas hunter Two Hawks squatted on the dense grey mud that fringed the shining disk of Matagorda Bay, watching two shore crabs rise out of their holes, seeming to taste as well as see the humid summer day with their eye-stalks. He remained motionless, still as the drifted buttonwood nearby, as the minutes passed, and gradually the crabs crept closer, closer, until one began pinching at the thick leathery sole of his foot that was deeply cracked by rough ground and salt marsh.

He smiled slowly at the pinch of the crabs, knowing how they waited, something always waited to feed as others fell. Soon, little brothers, he thought, and turned at the sound of gunfire, boom, boom, boom, boom, breaking the stillness of the day, and the crabs shot back into their holes as his toes gripped the broken shells in the mud and he raised his black eyes, one clouded over now, a haze on his right side that had begun three months ago.

Across this pocket of the bay, to the east a cloud of egrets and storks rose into the bright morning haze, but numbers fluttered back to earth, like handfuls of white flower petals between the fingers of a palsied hand. Boom, boom, boom, boom, the faint percussions drifted over the impassive mud flats. The feather hunters were stuffing their bags, he knew.

"I remember," he said aloud, a green heron cocking its head at the sound, one long leg poised to step further into the warm water, toes spread.

And he thought back through all those rounds of seasons, friends long dead or drifted to the whites, or further back into the stony wild that was beyond the monks and the mesquite. He remembered when he had begun to think about the sounds his father and mother sometimes made together in the woven reed dwelling and he had looked at the girls, at their bodies, in a new way. They had lived further north then, and he had looked across the water there on the upper reaches of Galvez where the bright birds floated down onto the islands to the east, the low islands that stretched into the Gulf and kept the waters quiet where their people fished and gathered oysters and crabs. He told his father he wanted to go out to the islands, paddle out there and catch some birds, for meat, he had said, but knew he wanted to make a feather bonnet for the girl on the other side of the clearing who looked at him with soft brown eyes and made him look away.

His father had looked hard at him, deep into the boy's eyes, and had said, "We will go and see the old man tomorrow," nodded, squeezed the boy's shoulder, and strode away.

The following morning, his father shook him awake and they walked out into the dark morning of the season before the long heat, the bushes and sawgrass dripping in the dawn, made water together near the edge of the clearing, and came back to the cold fire, filling pouches with smoked mullet and berries that hung over the coals. The stream water was cool to their throats, and they rose and followed the hard path that led south.

Just before noon, he followed his father down a side trail to the east and, leaving their pouches and knives, all but two bags made of knotted vine, they waded into the still waters in the lee of a finger of low sand. Schools of mullet jumped lazily, one darted in a curled vee beyond the reach of some prowling shark. The boy and his father began to feel forward with their feet, soon encountering the encrusted beds of oysters in the warm waist-deep water. According to the instructions of his father, they gathered four handfuls each of the fat shells long as their open hands and waded ashore. "For the old one," his father said, and the two continued their pace south.

Past an old red oak, its trunk disfigured like the hind leg of a deer that had been broken and mended poorly the boy had stalked and shot with his bow in the last frozen rain, his father's stick-straight back and tireless stride shifted west, seemingly into the midst of the dense palmettos and scrub oaks. At first, the boy had difficulty picking out the trail, so overgrown it was, but he soon began to notice up-croppings of limestone and harder rock among the fallen branches, rock that was polished smooth by the soles of passing feet, and the boy felt a brush of fear, as when last spring a panther's print in the fresh mud filled with water as he watched.

His father pushed on, rapidly, driven in a way the boy was not accustomed to, until after the trail circled around two hackberry trees draped in wild grapes, the trail widened to a clearing painted suddenly crimson and gold as the sun plunged down.

In the dying light, at the clearing's edge rose a mound of whitened oyster shell, tall as a man, and near the center of the grass-tufted clearing, next to a ring of smooth and tight-fitting fire stones, sat the old one.

After the sparks caught the moss tinder and sent tiny tongues of flame up into the twigs, catching twisted grey branches alright, the old man accepted the bags of oysters with a nod and carefully laid out the swollen shells in a row. He then brought a curious copper tool like a sharpened thumb out of a beaded pouch and began to pry open the shells, each with a hollow pop that made the boy's mouth run with saliva.

But as the man worked, the boy shyly stole glances at this old one they had traveled to see, but the man did not look like the old ones he had seen among his people, and this was certainly not a white old one, either. Chapetyl, his father had called him, was the color of oiled cedar, dark reddish brown, with thick grey strands of hair falling only below his ear under a curious collection of bright red and green and yellow feathers bound to his head in a manner the boy had never seen. Most odd was the man's face, round jaw, receding chin, jutting lips and thick hooked nose, like a stone hatchet, the man's face was, the eyes glittering black and shining, like the tiny arrow points he had seen from the south.

They ate, almost drank, the sweet oyster meats in the cooling dark around a yellow ring of flickering light, ate in silence, each buried in his own thoughts, the boy noticing as the flames began to crackle and blink green and red and blue, wondering if the salt caused that, when his father broke the night.

"The boy wants to go to the islands, after the birds."

"Humph," the man grunted, looking like one of the sad giant turtles that dragged themselves sometimes up onto the sand. He seemed to become one of these wrinkled creatures, opening his beak and beginning: "The storm god gathers the feathers of those birds for his cloak. You see them on some days sweeping the highest part of the sky, out of reach.

"There was a season long ago when the large birds lived here with us on the shore and we shared the fish and the crabs and the storm god came sometimes to gather his feathers but we knew him. But then came a people who killed, a people who killed people and birds and animals with little cause, who took birds with arrows and crept up onto the birds' nests in the dark and grabbed the birds by their long legs and killed and ate the tiny young birds until the birds cried out, screamed out loud and long for the storm god to help them.

Far to the south, in the southern sea where the water is warm as blood, the sleeping storm god raised his heavy eyes and heard the screams and cries of his beloved birds, and he arose and called to his great black thunder bird that carried him over the water, his bird

88

Hurakan, and the storm god grew sad and then angry as he listened, so that he grew darker and swelled and lightning bolts broke from his brow and torrents of tears poured from his eyes...."

The boy had been staring into the colors of the crackling fire but looked up at the old man, whose words were pounding out as steadily as the beating of a drum but his lips no longer moved and his eyes stared straight ahead into the night.

"And Hurakan rose and spread his black wings and began to beat them, the powerful feathers rending the sky, the air pushing the water into sharp peaks broken with white foam, and the storm god rode north on Hurakan, slowly, feeling the powerful muscles of his carrier beneath him, driven by the cries of the herons and storks, the egrets and terns that echoed across to expanse of the Gulf."

Again the boy raised his eyes and dimly saw the old man across the fire, his hard face shining, lips pressed together in anger, but the darkness throbbed with his voice, held the boy like hands pressing his shoulders down, his bare flanks feeling the broken shell and coarse sand imprinting his skin. His father sat motionless next to him, eyes closed, palms open on his knees, mouth hung loose at rest.

"The people who lived with the birds felt the sky hold its breath, saw the pelicans staying close in and low and looked out over the still water turning flat and grey. Far to the south at the edge of sight they saw the darkness spreading across the rim of earth, sweeping forward. As the day drew to a close they saw the wings of Hurakan black and tattered tearing across the sky and felt the anger of the storm god and were afraid.

All that night and into the following day the storm god held Hurakan hovering, panting, beating its terrible wings upon them and the storm god cried for his birds. The huge wings of Hurakan pushed and swept the waters of the Gulf up onto the land, far back into the land, until the people climbed high into the trees. Many of the new people did not know Hurakan, did not understand the water, and were drowned or were swept hard against the trees until their bodies broke, found later like old blankets draped over limbs..

On the afternoon of the second day, the storm god grew tired of his anger and turned his great bird and bid it to beat its wings back into the Gulf. As Hurakan withdrew, beating and pulling his great black wings, the waters fell, but as they fell Hurakan gathered and pushed back the land into the Gulf with his thick wings and clawing feet until all along the shore but separated from the land by shallow water Hurakan build up a row of islands from the mud and sand he had dragged back and made a home for the birds of the storm god.

As the last long pinions of Hurakan's plumes receded that afternoon, the storm god opened his colored cloak and let beams of sunlight burn down onto the new islands off the shore to show the birds the way, and they came and began to pace and strut and probe about in the mud and sand as the sun came out brilliant and sparkled on the glittering sea. The islands smoked and steamed in the sun like loaves of browned maize. The storks looked one to another as others wheeled down and wagged their thick heads, egrets strutted in the drying pools and with the herons speared frantic fish and slid them down long throats, ruffling their plumes contentedly. Far overhead the sandhill cranes circled and called to their far away homes. Terns chattered and probed the fresh sand with their sensitive beaks, and all the flocks knew the islands were their home, knew the storm god had heard their cries."

As the last droning fall of Chapetyl's voice was absorbed into the night, the boy looked up over the red and grey broken coals from the fire and saw the old man nod forward onto his chest, his necklace strands of pink and yellow shells glowing dully in the gloom. An immense fatigue swept over the boy, and his arms wrapped his knees, asleep before his forehead rested.

The dawn light wakened the boy, and he unfolded awkwardly, feeling the slick damp of the salt-coast air clinging like grease to his limbs, his hair wet to the touch. The fire was cold, and squatting on his hams next to the boy sat his father, impassive, almost amused.

"Where is the old man?" The boy asked.

"He has gone away."

"But where? Did you see him go?"

His father stared hard at him, turned down the corners of his hard mouth in what he felt a smile, and said "You know."

The boy had known, and the understanding made him glad that he soon would be a boy no more, and sad as the weight of knowledge sometimes settles on one's shoulders like a heavy burden, a bag of stones.

Two Hawks heard, far off, the boom of the feather hunters' guns, but thought instead they were the distant thunder of another storm and he smiled, as his father had, turning down the corners of his mouth. He did not feel the pinch of the crabs this time, did not feel the tiny claws pry open the cracks on his toes, did not see the bright red beads of blood as they tasted.

Wind

Privacy
Octavio Quintanilla

> *Todo quiere ser agua*
> Efraín Bartalomé

You wait a whole life to live through a hurricane
& then an entire city thirsts

Through a hole on the roof the clouds watch you
Move from room to room
As you scratch your head & try
To put wailing children to sleep

It feels like a village in this house
Where six of you are convinced
That you can be transformed

But till then
The days are humid & when night seeps in
You pass food by candlelight

There are no more stories to tell
No clear maps & no time you can remember
When the word *nostalgia* did not fit dreadfully
In the scheme of your life

The rain, you think, is an indecipherable gallop
That no one can tell if it arrives or if it recedes

It soaked the sofas & the mirrors
& the scruples you struggled to keep dry inside your coat

For now it's here
Among the amputee & the young bride
Among the children & the light's bruised vulva

In Texas, there's an excess of doors, you say, & nowhere to go
You want to blame something, someone,

But without a roof you hold it all in
& watch the lactating stars remind you

That unlike God who can't escape his godliness
You leave all flesh on a coat-hanger.

1956: The Sand Storm at Fort Stockton
Alan Birkelbach

It came straight across west,
brown like dry creek bottom,
like the tree trough where the springs used to be,

and swallowed the mountains first,
because it was still hungry from
drought-stricken Van Horn,

and we all watched it,
our Fords lined up on the edge of town,
engines pointed east in case we misjudged the speed.

Col. Warren had been out here first
because he'd been on the short-wave
listening to the pilots.

He'd been stationed in China
for years and had settled at Fort Stockton
after he retired because he said it was the biggest patch

of ground that most resembled the Gobi
that still had water.
We were waiting for the animals next.

White tail and jackrabbit and
prairie dogs didn't mean much
but whoever saw the first snake heading our way

was supposed to give up a yell
because that meant that the first blast of hot wind
was not more than a minute behind.

It was a matter of watching too close
but being in the wrong place
because we all looked over together when that sand slammed into us

And there was Col. Warren dressed down to his skivvies
for chrissakes, turned into the wind,
his arms stretched out, yowling his head off

straight out of the Mongolian horde,
and there was an army of snakes already
fifty yards beyond him heading for town ahead of us,

and we left him behind like we always did, cursing him a blue streak,
the sand faster than us, burning the backs of our ears,
taking the finish off our paint and chrome.

Port Bolivar after Hurricane Ike

Carol Coffee Reposa

I've come to see her
One more time,
This wrinkled diva
With a giant heart.
I want to hear it beat,
To touch that face
That shines for miles.

Generous and sloppy,
She slings iridescent baubles
Everywhere she goes, a parade queen
Throwing candy to the throngs,
Or conjures ribs in sand, scatters
Conch shells east and west,
Festoons the world in kelp.

Sometimes she turns moody,
Rages, spits out torrents
Shreds her belongings,
Tears things
To splinters,
Even feeds
On her young.

But then as suddenly
She stops,
Resumes her usual largesse
Smiles her glittering smile
And rubs
The world's back
Until it sleeps.

Wildness
Charles Inge

A wildness of wind
   and water is
in our lives today,
   with wind in wintry
gusts roiling the bay,
   the water leaden
the sky gray,
   and workboats tied
against the lee;
   gulls cry and slide
sideways to the wind,
   geese, a skein,
with haunting calls
   penetrate the air,
southward on their way;
   whitecaps top the waves,
the water's turned
   to spume . . .
there's a wildness
   in our lives today.

The Wind Relentless
Charles Inge

The wind
   intense,
now three days,
   limbs
and leaves
   torn away.

The sound
   outside
buffets the ears,
   inside
sounds like
   the sea.

Wind chimes
   clang crazily,
yard cans and chairs
   blown about,
plants and grass
   wither and dry.

Our great heron
   sweeping by
barely manages
   to keep on course—
the wind relentless
   three days now.

Tornado Alley

Chera Hammons

It's a house-shaker, cellar-thumper,
the sort that we are warned about,
but not all of us have basements
so we fit into our closets when it comes,
just widened-out eyes and elbows while
the outside air boils and sings with electricity.

We grow up with it, always know this might
happen to us, that we will sit in our groaning box
in a sea of wind, and will wait under pillows
that must stop whatever pieces of cars pierce the walls,

so we have planned ahead, know the safest room.
We know that while we wait
the rebar will be ripped from the concrete,
the studs will be stripped, sand-blasted with topsoil,
hail will beat the nearly-wild roses flat.
The bells at the non-denominational church
will clang like mad yelling saints, the power will flicker,

the lights may go out, the garage door thrown off
so the house is a vacuum, but the warning sirens
are always a thrill when they start up,
the way that families freeze to listen at first.
They pause in their meals, or their small talk,

and suddenly hear tree branches already
slapping the dust off their houses, and the spitting rain
that saturates the brick red like when it was new,
the windows rattling, and the mile-long rumble
that might not be a freight train.

We know more about meteorology than most.
A ridge of low pressure, straight line winds,
gulf moisture were in our bedtime stories.
The storm will pass soon, the worst ones
wear themselves out fast with their violence,

and the morning will sparkle with dew and bent metal,
the roots of the cottonwoods like old fingers
finally holding the sky like something they'd hoped for.

We have rebuilt now so many times that nobody thinks
it is unusual if you never find some of what blew away.
We will go outside to see what still stands,
meet our neighbors assessing the storm,
and what the new day is like, preening in its calm;
we'll call it a good day for repairing the damage,
a good thing that things were not worse.
The weather is our culture, what we have in
common, all we really know how to talk about.

Dust Devil
Chris Ellery

in memory of Buddy Holly

We chased dust devils in the Texas heat
My brother Buddy and me
Swirling phantoms of dusty heat
He seemed to know where they'd be

Over cotton patch stubble blue sky spread
The boy would look for the wind and wait
It seemed to pass right through him Buddy said
With its grit and its light and its heat

Air that fierce can scatter horses flatten barns
Buddy held it in
But when he played his playing was a storm
His song a wind

Over cotton patch stubble the Texas sky spread
Buddy would look for the wind and wait
It seemed to pass right through him he said
With its grit and its light and its heat

Up north the snow drifts clog the passes
The tour's gone cold as the weather
Buddy dreams of a summer in Texas
The music crickets make by rubbing legs together

The breeze swirls over the dust
Where the cotton has just been cut
Over the dryness the devil stirs
Through stubble and stones and burrs

Every day the stones cut deeper
The devil must be chased
The wind that slams you also lifts you
Out here we call that grace

Over cotton patch stubble blue sky spreads
Buddy looks for the wind and waits
The devil just passes right through him he says
With its grit and its light and its heat

Me and Dust Storms
Chuck Taylor

Did you ever do the dust thing?
Dust thing not out of the depression
Dust bowl with the Okies heading
In their junky Model T's for the green
Of golden seacoast California

No, not that, but the dust right
Here in flat West Texas. I bought
A used Plymouth once. It seemed
Fine until I drove it into the sunset
And discovered that the front

Windshield had been pitted by
Hard blowing tiny knives in
A dust storm, and facing the sun
I couldn't see a darn thing out
That front window now glinting

Light in all directions out of
Cut holes like tiny stars. You'd
Rush home as you saw a spring
Dust storm on the horizon humping
In, you'd carry a folded hanky

In your back pocket to cover
Your mouth and save your
Precious lungs if you got stuck
Outside. I felt I was on the lucky
Side wearing glasses to save

My eyes from the nasty grit. Inside
Your home, you'd look out from
A window and wonder why and
How this could be happening,
And somehow the dust would

Find a way to slip around your

Sealed windows. You'd see it
In the air floating down to gather
On the sill, and you'd step back,
No, not ready yet for dust to dust

Waiting Inland for the Hurricane
J. Todd Hawkins

In the morning, gray and distant,
there will be coffee and the waves
of a child's laughter when the images
of inundation give way
to Saturday morning cartoons.
Then, they say, will come the wind, rain.

We will putter nervously, bearing
the uneasy silence of pretended calm
as we hang old sepia family pictures
in the stairway.

Those grim faces from behind decades
of storms and loss will stare
and judge their progenies' faith.

We will know the places they show
on the news. We will have strolled
their sunny seawalls and tasted their ice creams,
soft like rainbows must be.

We will know it is futile to tie this world together
with chain link fences and swing sets.

Perhaps we will lose the young oak
we struggled all summer to free of fungus.
Perhaps we will lose more.

But now, the house only sleeps
and the wind chime
only whispers the delicate peals
of painful anticipation.

Water
Kurt Heinzelman

does that—
assumes the
shape of
other things

even when
attaining a
level all
its own

its beauty
a kind
of trickery

We love
things we
can understand

like water's
filthy green
sky before
a hurricane

Night Storm

Laurie Kolp

One night a hurricane
blows through
without warning.
Well, the 10:00 weatherman
predicts thunderstorms
says perhaps a small
tropical disturbance
might form overnight
but a much too recent
false-alarm evacuation
leaves us doubtful.
Soon branches thrash
against our windows
sheets of rain rattle
the eaves. 2 a.m.
Husband and I
open our eyes
and cuddle close.
One thing leads
to another—
who cares
about the weather?

Back to Some Beginning
Nathan Brown

Hurricane Ike blew her up I-45
from its dark eye over Houston
and into my hard-weathered arms.

We held each other in the cool sweat
of a cloudy Oklahoma sunset, riding out
the wide meteorological mood swings
of another fussy September night.

Then, we lay down to sleep there
in the doldrums of better dreams,
while the storm leveled Galveston,
trying not to think about how it is
that every once in a while nature
breaks out a can of turpentine
and wipes down the canvas,
returning every inch of it
to a primordial wash
of grays, browns,
and blues.

The Storm Cellar
Paul Ruffin

> To Walt McDonald,
> in memory of his storm cellar

Those green summer afternoons
when writhing fingers dance
across the Texas plains
my family will huddle here.

We gave up an apple tree and pear
to have this maw of concrete and steel:
It waits obscenely, its raw
back a gray hump on the lawn.
When green waves of wind fling
against the ribs of our house
and dash the heavens down,
our fate will lie in that damp belly
where we will be swallowed and saved
for a brighter day: thrown up
weak and short of breath, wet
with fear, but glad of this gray beast
and what is left to be counted and kept.

Beach Norther
Sally Ridgway

The house shakes on its stilts. Fine sand hisses
from the north, shimmers over dunes. Surf slams

the seaweed banks, willets bathing in new tidepools.
Overnight a leap from spring to fall, skipping

summer. All spring's dilemmas now resolved—
my stepson's illness, my daughter's job. I'm looking

back already or forward to new issues. All my agonies
and ecstasies (the sky is quivering) now equalized

by wind. Why have them at all? Why not just
eat and sleep? My meditation place at the dune line's

awash with fine new sand in ripples. Sand crabs' holes
filled, now seaweed crabs across the beach.

Between my lotus legs a new dune forms.

Wind Farm near San Angelo

Stan Crawford

From Africa, plumes of Saharan dust
blow all the way west into the Gulf
of Mexico, cast their dulling film upon
the glare-glass skyscrapers of Houston

and push north, rolling across the high plains.
From dry-farmed fields near Abilene
and Lubbock, native brick-red dust, aroused,
rises up to mingle with the foreign clouds.

Yucca and agave thrust their bladed leaves
like knives into the wind. There is no good
offense against the sandy dust, nothing that could
come to the rescue of the Dairy Queens,

the clapboard churches and small houses huddled
down before the storm. Over these victims loom
white giants, eight or ten, their wind blades smooth
and smoothly plowing through the muddled,

howling air, like lances slicing up the atmosphere.
Windmills and knights, combined within a single form.
But no one merely human goes out in the storm.
Some drink. Some pray. Some sleep and dream
that soon the price of oil will rise, the skies will clear.

March Blizzard, Amarillo
Steven Schroeder

Half a mile to the end
of the city, where there is nothing
but north and four strands of barbed wire.

Walk it, and you know
it's the wind not the snow
that drifts knee high heavy.

West south east to where you began,
every new drift of this March blizzard waits
for morning's first footprints. Wind strips snow

to ice. Birds that were here a day before are gone,
but they will sing the day to mind again
when they come again tomorrow.

Texas Equinox
Sylvia Riojas Vaughn

Sirens wail.
My man steps
onto the porch.
Come see! he hollers
despite my whimpers.
I race to the bathroom,
quilt over my head.
Lightning cracks,
turns night into day.
Hailstones pelt the roof.
The wind picks up,
tosses iron patio furniture.
Forty minutes later,
the fury passes.
The next door neighbor
loses his fence.
The couple
down the street,
their roof.
We count ourselves lucky,
only the grill's destroyed.
Some folks post photos
of the blazing night,
energy of nature;
I, serene scenes
of bluebonnets.

Autumn
William Virgil Davis

The oaks have been speaking Spanish all
afternoon. They do not want to die again,
but the first ripples of a winter wind came
in last night and they knew what that meant.
This morning when I walked out under them
they bent down to embrace me, shedding
leaves like summer rain all over the lawn.

A Winter Day
William Virgil Davis

We have been expecting snow.
It is late this year, but we know
it will come. We sit together
before a fire, watching the windows
blaze with reflected light,
speaking softly, sipping mulled
wine, watching and waiting.

Our windows frame the dark
and a whisper of wind teases,
then touches, the house. An owl
calls across the arroyo, once,
twice. And then the silence is
still all over again, as we wait
for winter to come, come in.

A Private Miracle
Jan Seale

When I think of miracles, I think of the one that happened to me when I was a boy of five.

As other children, I had my own fierce secret demons—beings I did battle with when I was alone on the dusty road between my house and the mailbox, or in the dark of my bed on the screened porch of our house in the middle of an orchard, or in the midst of my friends at the Head Start program where I went to learn English. Maybe I had more than my share because I did not have any brothers or sisters to divide the unknowable and secret world with.

I was not afraid of the usual things—my parents, the dark itself, death—though I had an inkling of death because there was no grandfather to match my grandmother, my dear *abuelita* who lived with my mother and father and me. No, my worst demons lined the boundaries, the fields and roads around our home deep in the Rio Grande Valley of Texas.

When the wind blew in from the Gulf, as it did most of the time, the regiments of giant palms looked out to sea, their headdresses lazing behind them. Times like that I dared to look up at them through slatted fingers. Yet their heads were so high I could see their tops only in silhouette against the sun-crazed tropical sky.

But when the wind came from the north, they took on the awesome personages of full-blown warriors, savages glaring down at me, pitching their wildest war dances and looking as menacing as the face on my Big Chief tablet.

It was on one of these gusty October days that I was sent to the mailbox a half-mile down the road, the last part of the way lined with the terrifying beings. I could not bear these mandatory excursions without my pet, a big green bottle I pulled behind me on a string. Perro had a knack for distracting me with squiggly lines in the sand as he followed me. Besides, he made me infinitely braver.

That day I did my usual ritual. Before I came to the palms, I stood in the red ant bed, sidling in so I wouldn't disturb them, then watching them explore new paths over my feet and legs. It is one of my earliest memories of *machismo*.

I led Perro to the side, coiled his string carefully, and said, "Be a good Perro! Wait right here!"

Then I turned up my collar, clamped my hands over my ears, and ran like the dickens past the huge gray feet of the warriors. Safely to the box, I put the letters between my teeth, spread the newspaper over my head, and headed back for Perro.

But a curious object stopped me on my way. I remember the shock of discovery as if it were yesterday. It seemed a large greenish-yellow fan had come to be lying in the road. I picked it up and turned it over and over, wondering why I had missed it going the other way. Perhaps I knew, deep down, that it had shaken loose from the trees above, but, charged as all the world was to me then, it was a gift and a mystery. My childish bent for innovation took hold and I remember saying softly, "I know what. I'll take this home to Abuelita."

So I tucked the fan under one arm, smoothed the teeth marks on the letters, re-folded the newspaper carefully, found Perro, and thought of a song to whistle as I approached the house.

My grandmother was sitting on the porch.

"Abuelita!" I called, running toward her. "Look what I brought you!"

"*Ah....gracias!*" she replied, with only a grandmother's intuition for what I thought its obvious use was. She took it and made wide sweeping motions before her face. "The afternoon is hot. A storm is coming."

That night, my mother and father left the TV on quite late to hear the weather bulletins. Papa hammered boards across the windows and Mama filled every pitcher and pan we owned with water. My grandmother laid out candles and matches.

Hurricane! It was a word of incantatory power, and a torment I shared with the grownups. I was afraid to go to sleep that night. "*Mamma-grande!*" I called, in the face of fear using the big name for her.

She appeared in the doorway, her gray hair framed in the light. "What, *mi hijo?*"

"Tell me about the hurricanes." To ask if this one would hurt me would not be brave.

She came to my bed and sat down. She took my hand and told me of all the hurricanes she had been through. At last she said, "I am very old. You can see that no hurricane has ever hurt me." It was as solemn a pledge to me as if she had been God.

I was glad I had found her the fan. I was glad she could tell good stories. I was glad she was old, for the trust I could place in her words.

118

Soon, and despite my pledge to keep a vigil, all the things I was glad of turned into sleep.

In the morning, the wind was blowing, blowing hard. The sky was green and gray and the sun seemed to have forgotten to come up. My mother would not let me go outside. She only let me stand on the porch and look out—and even then I had to peek between two boards to get a view of the savages.

They were doing a frightening dance. They pitched their bonnets across their faces, the feathers endlessly tormented by the terrible breeze, and bent farther over than I had ever imagined they could.

The wind blew all that day. It rattled the windows and sent pieces of the chicken house roof flying across the yard. It tore down the banana trees and picked all the leaves from the elm. A bale of hay went walking across the yard, end over end, like a yellow straw monster.

I slept with my grandmother that night. Sometimes now, dozing in a half-light, I can hear her say, "*Hijito*, it was hot with the windows closed. Did you see me fanning with my fan today?"

By morning the wind had stopped. Papa pried the boards off the windows. Mama looked out and observed that the hens had somehow survived. But then it began to rain. "In every hurricane I was ever in, it rained and rained and rained," Abuelita said.

My father cleared his throat. "I don't think I can get the truck down the road. It's too muddy. *Mihijito*, you'll be going for the mail."

I had a thousand excuses, none of which made it to my lips. I put on my boots and raincoat and Mama gave me a plastic bag for the letters.

I set out alone, without the company of Perro, who would only slow me down today. The ant bed was gone, washed away. Coquena, my pet guinea hen, sat in an old orange tree fluffing herself. The rain felt like thousands of needles. I kept my head down.

And that was a mistake. Suddenly I slipped. I started falling all over the road. Everywhere I tried to stand seemed unreasonable.

Finally I quit flopping about. I was sprawled on something as round and hard and huge as a giant's leg.

Slinging mud off my hands, I struggled to my feet and stared down at what had stopped me. It stretched almost to the mailbox. It was one of the warriors. I turned for home.

But a few steps back and I heard my father's voice in my head. "Why didn't you get the mail?"

So I turned once again and, taking the far side of the road, hurried on. The warrior stretched one, two...five orange tree rows long. And at the end lay its head, crashed against the mailbox.

There is a longing in us to touch our fears, to make them ours by knowing them in all their sting. I reached out and touched the war bonnet, that thing which up until this moment had been a dark terror above me in my childhood sky. And that is when I knew the heavy feathers of my phantom warriors were simply palm fronds—green, brown, yellow—exactly like the one I had given my grandmother.

If even the innocent sin, I must have felt somehow my sin against the trees. I had the urge to make peace. And so I stooped and put my arms around the fallen palm's neck. Of course my hands did not touch. And then I climbed up on it and, stretching full length, lay there a moment, a moment in time that is a frieze in my head—a boy resting the sweet fears of his small existence on a tree fallen to earth.

From here on, the story is but a blessing and an amen to the miracle. The next day when I went for the mail again, the sky had brightened. The trees in the orchard dripped rain from their waxy leaves and ants crawled around, reviewing the damage to their mound. The road-repair people had come early that morning and taken away the fallen warrior.

I remember, when I came to the palms, stopping, and, halting Perro behind me, looking straight up at the trees. They were gazing benignly out toward the ocean again, their motion lazy and gentle.

"Hello, all you!" I shouted. And then I turned to Perro to see if he'd like to accompany me the whole distance.

He hesitated, that I remember.

"There's nothing to be afraid of," I said.

So he came with me, making new lines in the fresh wet sand.

Don't Know Why, No Sun Up in the Sky
Chuck Taylor

The rains were slashing, I could see, looking out the Galvez window. The wind was howling around the corner of the building, which held solid, and the thunder was blasting. The night was black, and except for the flashes, I could not see through the heavy downpour, beyond the curved concrete seawall, to the churning ocean.

I've been in big storms in Galveston before. In one storm we parked in the Kroger parking lot and the winds shook our old Winnebago so much we worried it would flip over. The water leaked in around the windows. A small mongrel dog, soaked and cold, gave up, crouching and shivering in the middle of the abandoned asphalt. I got myself soaked trying to bring the dog into our RV, but he would have none of it, and scampered off. All I got for my efforts was a cold. The radio in our RV was not working, so we rode the storm out on the blind faith that it was not a dangerous tropical storm or a hurricane. Police cars with blue lights flashing would have driven around this close to the ocean if terrible events were in the making.

Galveston Island, fifty miles south of Houston—a barrier island just off the coast—had not been overcome by water since the 1900 hurricane, when the raging sea swept over the whole of the island. Here it was March of 1998 and the island had not been submerged by a hurricane since.

Yet one always worried.

My wife Janine and I were in town for our 30th wedding anniversary. We hoped, as many couples do, that the trip would provide a bit of a romantic pickup for our marriage—a marriage that seemed to have lost its way since our daughter left and moved to New York City for the arts and culture. Our twenty year old hoped to become an actress but so far waited tables.

This Saturday night however we were stuck in front of the TV following the storm, wondering if we'd be able to get off the island on the bridge Sunday to get back to San Antonio for work. Janine taught dance; I was an elementary school principal.

We were watching a Houston station that had good weather reporting technology—Doppler radar, for instance—when suddenly images of Star Drug jumped on the screen. Star Drug in old downtown Galveston, said to be the oldest drugstore in Texas, was burning. Flames leaped off the roof.

"We've been there," Janine said. "It was empty of things to buy. All they had was sandwiches and drinks at the soda fountain. Do you remember the waitress getting angry at you?"

"No," I said.

"You started asking her all sorts of questions about the history of the drug store she didn't know. She was busy. You made her feel stupid."

"I don't remember."

"I'm not surprised."

"Memory is selective," I replied. "We've stayed at the Hotel Galvez three times. What do you remember of the elevator we came up?"

"It has metal walls."

"That's not much. It's an elevator of historical significance."

"Quit playing professor."

"They built that elevator for President Franklin Roosevelt when he came to Galveston. He was in a wheelchair and wouldn't fit in the regular one."

"Mr. Professor."

"I'm trying to show you memory's selective. We remember what we care about."

"And you forget when you're being stupid."

"Let's watch what's going on outside."

"If we hadn't done it before marriage, and you'd used condoms, we'd not had our daughter so early and maybe you could have become a history professor instead of boring yourself being a principal."

"So you're blaming me for our child."

"I'm not blaming you. I'm stating a fact."

"That building's torched. It looks like all that will be left is the brick and mortar."

"It's depressing. Why don't you turn it off?"

"We've got to watch this storm."

"Ninety-eight years and no big gully washers. Relax. We've done this before. Let's go down to the bar. It'll make us feel better."

"We have to watch."

"They have TV."

"They'll be watching sports, Janine."

"I'm going to the bar."

I stayed and watched more of Star Drug burning, and then watched the weather report on the storm. All the Houston channels were claiming this storm would probably bring no serious flooding, and that the Galveston sea wall would not be heavily breached. I didn't know whether to believe them, since weather reporters in Texas come out dead wrong half the time, but Janine had been gone for an hour and I thought I better go down to make sure she wasn't getting totally plastered.

Janine had been emotionally off during our four-hour drive from San Antonio. She has never liked the slow way I drive, but I'd already paid for the hotel and was not in any big hurry. 'More tailgaters,' she'd point out. 'Somebody's going to run into our rear end. You see how they storm around us. They're mad."

'I'm doing the speed limit,' I replied, keeping eyes steady on Interstate 10.

I went down to the bar and looked for Janine. The place was medium sized and dark. The heavy carpet needed a cleaning. I ordered a beer and sat down at a spot at the bar with a view of the women's rest room. I could have sat by one the large front windows and watched the palm trees in front of Hotel Galvez whip around in the storm, but what if the windows blew out? I wanted to spot my wife as she came from the lavatory. Janine can take sometimes up to twenty minutes to refigure her makeup in a mirror, so I settled in for the long haul, working slow on one of those generic American beers that taste like cow piss. After forty minutes I became a tad worried and raised my hand to signal the bartender.

"Have you seen a tall thin woman wearing pink pants and a pink t-shirt? I asked. "She's got short white hair."

The bartender didn't look at me. He was busy washing beer glasses in the sink below the bar. All he did was stick the beer glasses in the soapy water upside down, shake them in the suds, and then rinse them off. I wondered if the water contained a bit of bleach. The bar was almost empty, and he was watching the weather instead of sports. Once and a great while you run into a bartender capable a modicum of smarts. A year back on Sixth in Austin I'd talked to a graduate student gal in a nice low cut thing that was a classics' major at the University of Texas. She had mastered Latin and Greek. She had read Herodotus

"Well," the bartender finally said. "It's not our job to do anything more than keep track of how much people drink, so they don't drive home drunk."

"My wife doesn't drive. She works as the driver critic. We're staying at this hotel. I haven't seen her in an hour and a half and I'm worried that something might have happened."

"What can I say? I don't mean to be insulting, but you could be a stalker for all I know."

"Do you want me to call the police and have them come?"

The bartender paused. "If you can bring the desk clerk here, to prove that you both checked in, maybe I can look through the receipts and tell you something."

"OK," the bartender said when I got back with the desk clerk. "Your wife ordered three margaritas with salt on the rim. She did sit at the bar. I remember now the pink. She didn't say anything besides ordering drinks."

"Does the receipt tell when she left?"

"Let's see. Yes, it does. She left at 9:15. When did you order your beer?"

"Around 9:30. She didn't go outside in this storm? I'm worried about her."

"No. I can tell you she did not go out in the storm."

"Where did she go? Did she go to the basement to look at the history displays? We've always been interested in the one you have on when the mob ran Galveston."

"I didn't pay attention to where they went."

"You just said 'they'. She left with someone?"

"We like to respect the privacy of our guests, sir."

"OK. I'm calling the police."

"She left with a man, sir."

"How the hell do you know?'

"He paid for her margaritas."

"I know you've got a lot of young beach bum gigolos in town who prey on older women."

"I don't know anything about that."

"Oh come on. You work in a bar. You know what goes on."

I went back to the desk clerk. I then talked to the hotel management. Everyone gave me the same line. It would be a violation of privacy laws if they gave me his name, and they didn't know for sure his name, just a nickname, Bud. It was like giving a stranger in a bar someone else's credit card number or social security card. I told them I was a respectable school principal and owned no guns. I thought what they were saying was bullshit, but decided to go back to the room and contact a lawyer friend back in San Antone, and then call the police. I rode back up to the fifth floor in Franklin Roosevelt's famous elevator, worried about my wife, and wondering why no plaque had been mounted inside or by the elevator.

The TV was on when I got back to the room. Mostly they continued to report on the storm but they'd cut over to Star Drug fire now and then. They started saying the storm would not rate as tropical when it made full landfall. I walked over to the phone and noticed a small green light on its face blinking. I pushed zero for the front desk.

"You have a message, sir."

"Who is it from?"

"I don't know. A woman. Perhaps your wife."

"It's for me. What does it say?"

"I don't know, sir. Mrs. Knowles, I assume. The other desk clerked folded it and put the note in your box. We don't read the messages of our guests. You'll need to come down and show us your driver's license, as you did when you checked in."

"I just talked to you."

"The phone, sir. I can't recognize for certain your voice."

"Jesus Christ," I swore, and immediately regretted it. I knew you weren't supposed to take the Son of God's name in vain here in Texas, or anywhere in the South, but I was rattled.

Still in the room, I surmised that whatever the note said, it was not happy news. The rain and winds were still carrying on like crazy outside. I stared for a while out the window into the dark to settle myself, and then sat down on the bed in front of the television.

Why go down for the note? I had enough stormy weather. The sky ought to be clearer in the morning.

Riding the Wind
James Hoggard

North Texas weather guarantees adventure. Some say we don't really have seasons here, we have erratically spaced endurance tests. Others say nature's a prankster with a bias for the vicious—or the thrilling—depending on the amount of porcelain in your crop. The land is expansive but scarcely susceptible to terms of endearment, unless they're delivered with prickly obliqueness, the way natives here often address each other. "The place scares me," I've heard new residents from the East say. "The emptiness of it goes on forever. It makes me feel like I'm lost on the ocean. Do you ever get used to it?"

The answer, of course, is no, though I usually don't explain that terms associated with the benign or malignant are no more appropriate for defining it than are straight lines for describing the directions truth takes. Winters are not dependably cold, except ordinarily in February, when it's bitterly cold, and now and then in mid-September when it's not even autumn; and Christmas days outdoors are as likely to require mere shirtsleeves as they are overcoats and gloves. Summers, of course, are always hot; however, they, too, provide ranges of sensations. Variations in breezes and humidity can make thermometers irrelevant for measuring discomfort. Years ago, for instance, two cousins of mine from Wisconsin swore one July in the backyard after badminton that they were about to faint from the heat. At the same time, my brother, who was shivering, ran inside for a jacket.

He might have been teasing them. We often refuse to acknowledge when we're joking, a regional trait, as many newcomers learn. The texture of egg on the face makes entertaining designs, even for the butt of the joke when he learns that the delight comes from playing with truth and illusion much more than from hostility. Surfaces, one learns, are often misleading. Tennis at 105 degrees sometimes makes more sense than it does on days when the temperature is only in the mid-90s. If you don't like the weather, as the old saw says, hang around—it'll change in a bit. The changes, however, have their effects.

Late nineteenth century pioneers—their images surviving in photographs—often look as demented as they do coldly fierce. One reason for that is their scorched pale eyes whose sober stares say that some of them, stricken by terrible winds, went insane. But they always looked interesting to me; they seemed wonderfully ghostly in their attitudes of silent defiance, and certainly more interesting than I, as a child, ever thought I could be. Only later did I learn what tricksters and hellions many of them had been. But by then I was past what the ignorant call innocence. I had begun to appreciate the wiliness of scrawny coyotes, the subtly mad beauty of mesquites, the delightfully sensual shapes revealed in cumulonimbus clouds—it made no difference after awhile that thunderheads rarely delivered rain. After all, I was learning—from reading things other than *My Weekly Reader*—that even Zeus had often ranted and raved for no good purpose, like some of the adults whose company I got subjected to in the parsonage. There were advantages to becoming half-pagan, I would learn, unmindful of the fact that spring and fall winds were giving me instruction, along with useful distractions from self. The sudden changes in weather had also opened others to wonder and cunning; the two aren't necessarily alien to each other, I keep discovering.

Walking home from school when I was a child, I was sometimes unable to see across the street because the sky was wild with a red dust curtain. My face was stinging, my throat and nostrils were raw, and walking demanded a fight. Even then, with nothing to be nostalgic about, I found the time exciting. The violence of the weather was thrilling. The dust has not blown as thickly since, I think, but the winds still generate a gloriously pagan strength; and if the turbine vents on roofs aren't tied down, they often go out of balance. The sound of their whirling, drilling through beams and sheetrock, becomes so loud the top of the house threatens to fly away. There is nothing nice about that noise, especially when it comes in the middle of the night as one tries to find rooms which are quiet enough for sleep. Being a pilgrim in one's own home doesn't help satisfy the craving for rest.

Hearing the windblasts tonight, I recalled two recent springs. They came back to back, and I wasn't prepared for either, though both of them did me good. The lessons they taught, however, were something other than lyrical and clearer than the gimp-legged rhythms of our seasons. One involved an ambiguous return home from Europe; the other involved an explosion in the environment, a miracle of disaster which could only be redeemed by a change of perception, although twelve months separated them, memory puts those two times together. On the flight back from Europe, my wife and I stopped for two days in Iceland. A delay, I thought, would soften the blow of the return. But it didn't.

Leaving the Dallas/Fort Worth airport, I was appalled by the ugliness of the land. Even the weeds hadn't really turned green. The trunks of the scrawny trees were grayer than they were brown. A chilly wind howled; it whistled through the rented car's windows. I felt awful. A fine trip was over, and the place I was coming home to looked desiccated. Only the demented, I thought, would be stupid enough to live here. We didn't have to stay, though. Less than a month later we were leaving for several weeks in California. Frantic with defiance, however, I planted a garden first and said some words over the tilled spread I had sown and poked seeds in. I did not mutter a kind blessing. I said what I've often said after planting. I told the land and seeds that by god if they didn't become fruitful and multiply with embarrassingly ample fecundity I would kill them, rip the earth apart with my bare and blistered hands. A soft approach might be more fitting in the tropics or river bottoms, but where I live, belligerence, even if it's laughable, seems to work best.

One week later, my wife and I were relaxing. We were watching the evening news in bed. Walter Cronkite told us, "That's the way it is" for April 10, 1979, but the truth was just getting started. The sky was bleak and the winds were up. Two minutes after 6:00 p.m., the television set went off, along with everything else run by electricity. Warning horns were roaring. We went downstairs and saw a huge dark cloud in the west. We went out in the backyard to see it better. Broad and black, it was barreling toward us. I was sure it wasn't a tornado. Its breadth was too massive. As the winds turned fierce and large drops of rain began falling, we saw trees whirling around the edge of the cloud. My wife ran inside but I stayed to watch it. Hail began falling then I ran inside, too, but only to get my camera and put on a pith helmet. I ran back out and began to take pictures. Four tornadoes had joined, we later found out. They stayed together for miles. I ran to the side of the house to get better shots as the black mass began veering away from us three quarters of a mile away. Hail banged against my helmet. Fragments of ice bounced off the grass. I went back inside. We could only get one station on our portable radio. Finally the sky we saw through the windows began clearing, but night was falling. For a moment the twilight turned a sickly amber, then again became gray. The news we got between pop tunes was patchy. All electricity was off. The station was broadcasting now from its mobile unit.

We drove to check on my parents. Much of the roofing on their apartment complex was gone. Their living room windows were broken. My father said that from the balcony he had watched the tornado coming toward them, but when it hit the hillsweep in the ravine below them, it took a jigstep and leaped around them. They were lucky. Some large homes near them had been flattened. One of their neighbors, we found out several days later, had also been lucky. He was driving to the hospital to see his wife. Stopped at a clogged intersection, his car had been picked up and deposited in a shopping center's parking lot a quarter-mile away. He and the car had not been hurt, though with embarrassment he finally confessed, "I did—wet my pants."

Another person, whose car went sailing near his, didn't survive; and almost fifty others were killed that evening. Twenty thousand people, one-fifth of Wichita Falls, became homeless within a few minutes. There was no time to meditate on what had happened. One didn't know at that point the scope of the disaster. A man and his wife fled from a shopping mall for their car. As he glanced back to catch her hand, he found she was gone. It would be several days before workers found her body on top of a building miles away.

As if somehow prepared for such turmoil, the city didn't seem to panic. Friends and strangers worked through the night to help dig belongings out of rubble. Friends and acquaintances moved in with each other; and in the morning, when salvage work resumed, crudely painted signs, like flowers and weeds, appeared in the wake of the blast. Messages appeared on fragments of walls, on chimneys which looked like towers besieged. Notices sang off-key on boards anchored in debris. The water and electricity were still off. Telephones didn't work. Some of the signs, bearing names and addresses, said, *All safe.* Others told jokes: *Who says the Bakers don't throw wild parties?. . . Split level for sale cheap—part split, part level. . . . Spring cleaning and free a/c . . . It's our neighbors' damn mess—we're neat.* And then the inevitable zinger: *Where in the hell's Dorothy & Toto?* One thought of the Vikings, their habit of dying with jokes on their lips. One thought of frontiersmen playing on the plains. Some, though, were shy about drawing comfort from such comical outbursts. "Within six months, there'll be a lot of breakdowns," a minister told me after he'd met with other councilors. But there weren't nearly as many as predicted. The working continued. The city water, flowing now, was contaminated. Grocery stores gave away containers of distilled water trucked in, and barbecue pits and camping stoves, many learned, boiled water and cooked as well as electric ranges. Many gathered their water from swimming pools at motels. Side yards became toilets. "The shrubs are going to be nitrogen-drunk," a friend told me, deciding to forgo another breakfast beer.

The people were enterprising and usually polite. They obeyed with friendliness the civilian volunteers directing traffic. They did become cantankerous, however, when uniformed National Guardsmen took over; but then the people on the plains, like other Americans for more than two centuries, have traditionally balked and barked at authority. Still, there was little looting, and few went hysterical, though a number got nervous—some giddy—when blustery winds began blowing. Speeding through necessary tasks and finding again the thrill in cheerful cussing with friends who had become as hyperkinetic as I was, I began realizing I loved the place. My cringing the spring before on returning from Europe was changing. I felt like giving the place an *abrazo*, a big sloppy hug. My bones said, *Do it*, but my head said, *Get to work and quit playing.*

Several days later came Easter. Waiting for my wife to finish dressing for church, I went out in the backyard to see if anything in the garden had sprouted. I hadn't had time to water in almost a week. Unfortunately the nutgrass was thriving, but there wasn't anything useful growing except radishes.

I was thinking about my children who had finally managed to get us on the phone from Houston. Before they reached us—they'd been trying to call at least every five minutes, my son said; and my daughter told us the Red Cross had told her that someone with our name was dead. She yelled in outrage at the mistake. Many others, friends from across the country, also called—some I hadn't talked to in ten years. Our home became a gathering place. Quite often we had fifteen people for supper, some of them my wife had never seen before. Working on roofs, cleaning out a new friend's restaurant, tromping through riprap, I'd been free with invitations for dinner. The nights were full of celebration and, in different ways, the days were, too. Approaching the sheltered patio, I glanced at the base of a big fruitless mulberry. I saw something I had never seen before. Little white flowers, their petals describing stars, ringed the tree. The Stars-of-Bethlehem had bloomed.

The church was packed. Much of the congregation was in shirtsleeves. The membership had been hit hard. A lot of them were wearing most of the clothes they owned. The long lily procession began as the organ, playing Wagner's "Pilgrim's Chorus" from *Tannhäuser,* throbbed. All rose when the choir, having placed more than two hundred lily pots at the chancel began leading the rest of us in singing "Christ The Lord Is Risen Today." Voices began cracking. Tears began streaming down cheeks. I wiped my own away, but others replaced them. The arms of the minister of music slashed gloriously toward the arcing walls and groined ceiling above him. His wife's face shone as she sang. Two weeks before, the reconstruction and redecorating of their home, saved for for more than fifteen years, had been finished. The place was now trash, but they and the rest of us were discovering, as we wept and sang heartily, that the fact of resurrection is far more powerful than the tremors of sweet convention.

Then and later I began thinking about those populaters of the past who, through disaster, had lost faith in God and man—the one often a euphemism for the other—people whose dying hour was gloom, as Nathaniel Hawthorne had said about one who was an emblem of the many. I remembered Jean-Paul Sartre, brilliant and as wall-eyed as a mixed metaphor, saying that the holocaust of World War II was a sign that no worthy God existed, and probably no God at all. I remembered, at the other attitudinal extreme, my mother telling me decades before—during an argumentative period in my youth—that she didn't think she could stand to live if she didn't know there was a Heaven. I remembered others whose faiths seemed to have been shattered by catastrophes or created by luck. I also remembered that I had never seen any necessary connection between terror and purpose. It was clear why things like teleology and eschatology seemed to some like wool-gathering, the kind of project undertaken by someone late at night with nothing better to do than chatter. I was glad, though, to discover that few in our place had been inclined to bray about a relationship between bad weather and a displeased god. Even the idea of the Bible Belt as a peculiar region spasming overwhelmingly with fundamentalist claptrap seemed out of joint with what I was seeing; and that gave me pleasure. It was nice to see a wrong cliché smeared.

It was also necessary, then as well as now, to resist spewing sentimental pabulum. Language, whether spoken or written, is an organic force. It is not, as some would say, merely a series of tools or signs pointing to something over there outside ourselves. It is also prior to what we are, and beyond what we are. It uses us as much as we use it. In indirect ways the changeable weather reminded me of that. Faced with a dramatically changeable climate, I began to see more clearly why the people from the plains have prized restraint, except when they're out of their minds and frantic, as sometimes they are.

I began also to see why stories seemed to have meant more to them than abstract discourse. I began seeing why many students here— who weren't worth a flip handling writing assignments demanding classification, logical process, and comparison and contrast—excelled at narrative. Their parents and grandparents' conversation had often been full of stories, many of them simultaneously hair-raising and whimsical. On the plains, as a number of historians have realized, vitality was in greater demand than coherence; and the sensory dimensions of elements were of more than immediate interest than meaning, as indicated by the goofy spasms of voice and body encouraged by some of the more primitive religious sects; as also indicated by the adult chaperons of student trips—the more righteous the students' backgrounds, they've told me, the randier they are.

As it was then, so it is now: the world on the plains is vivid with texture, inhospitable though it often is. A yucca blade can lay open the skin as finely as a sharp knife, a fact familiar to anyone who's tried to pull johnson grass out of the fanning yucca plant. Even in a common yard one is likely to find throughout the year varieties of form, color, and texture in wild flora that prosper, tidy people discover to their distress, when and where they want: wild verbena, chickweed, bluebonnets, wild carrots, dandelions, goatheads, sweet clover, grass burrs, sunflowers, black-eyed Susans, mesquite, and mimosa shoots— and many other poor but hearty relatives of store-bought plants which, if not coddled, have the tendency to give up, lie down, and die, ungrateful for the abundance of clay which, it's been said, is as willing to give any creature as firm a foundation as concrete. There's an obvious parallel between the plants and people who thrive here, though perhaps there is not as much sameness in the rhythms of weather for the people to develop the peace of mind—and decency of conscience—necessary for contemplation. Bullshooting and spitting against the wind are quite different from extended meditation.

There is, however, the impulse to tell stories and spray opinions —and to contradict those same opinions in a moment—and not worry any more about consistency than nature does. Even those opinions, I begin to suspect, might be invalid impressions, might simply be another form of wind tunneling through the twisted troughs of imagination. I can't bring myself to call the people heroic or grand possessors of admirable character, not if I care anything about accuracy; and I certainly can't call the environment idyllic. It isn't even pretty, except in town after spring rains when, by chance, the lawns were mowed the day before, and the weeds still look like grass; and we, for a moment, try to convince each other that a sudden quarter-inch of spring rain indicates that the coming summer will be mild. There is one object, though, I can say is attractively poetic, an emblem of hope as well as a metaphor for reality: the mesquite.

Coming back to that tree—or is it a shrub?—I feel like a bee craving honeysuckle. The ridiculousness of the notion somehow seems reasonable. Its thin leaves lyrically graceful, the mesquite's body begins branching the moment it breaks earth. It seldom has a proper trunk. Hearty and resilient in its fiber and extroverted in its flare, it makes no wall against wind, a trait that often keeps it from breaking; and unless you're a jackrabbit, it won't give you much shade. Not even native to the area, it arrived somewhat more than a century ago, its seeds tangled in the hide of cattle, and also carried in their hooves and bowels. Demanding little water, it thrived; and its budding means spring has arrived, for although other plants and trees might get caught by late freezes, the big mesquites rarely bud until after last-frost, and most of the little ones don't either. It's canny that way. It's also restrained like a dry-witted prankster. Its coming out is not flashy with glory. Its delicate leaves and thin, irregularly turned limbs say, with a smirk, that it's ready for whatever foolishness—peaceful or terrible—nature has to offer; and its bark is tougher than the bark of its domesticated yard-dwelling cousin, the mimosa.

Its presence in the area roughly equals the age of the post-Indian settlements here. It looks indigenous, but it's not. Slyly fertile, it has a sparseness of line Oriental in effect, *sumi-e* in mode; and its thorns are emblems of violence. The violence, however, is more defensive than aggressive. In that it's different from the type of locust, which in swampy areas of, say, Louisiana, is called the thorn tree. The mesquite is the geo-spiritual sign of North Texas itself. It embraces the seasons, or what passes for seasons. It does so with grace, but with a slyness that's never fey. If to some it's a curse, to others it's a blessing. It's much like one of A.B. Guthrie's Indians: too polite a fellow to let on that you stink. It gives the impression of being receptive to the tremors and songs of earth and wind, but it's too wry to be called thrilling in appearance or sappily gracious. In that it's a mythic tableau for many of the people who become uneasy when faced with grand gestures of passion, whether affectionate or belligerent. Open to thrusts of wind, it provides no harbor. It calls to mind the restlessness of the life force itself. It calls to mind that the world is not as lush and coherent as we wish it were. But perhaps more than anything else, it calls to mind an openness that, while endless, is strangely depthless—what the Hindus have called the Void: the shapeless presence out of which all things emerge and into which all things go—including dreams, objects, truths, and lies.

Thinking about the mesquite, we pay attention to winds whipping dust all over the land; and seeing great spaces striated by thorny twigs, we see the young rage of another new year and are tossed about by its raw energy—a meteorological boiling that physicians and patients have observed coincides with an increase in gastrointestinal irritations and sinusitis. As the heavens go wild in spring and fall, the gut and head do, too.

Between the wild times comes summer with its enervating weight; and while lawns are turning to straw—they'll do it again in winter—and even weeds are shriveling, crepe myrtles bloom red, purple, and white. Spring is then over, and we forget that it wasn't a lyrical time. Errant, we remember it as balmy, cool, and moist. When the sunsets turn brilliantly orange and vermilion, we remember spring again and stir our sagging energy with fleeting reminiscences on its rough and barbaric winds. We might even miss them then and wish they were here—anything to shove away the heat. And perhaps for a moment, as the droughty scorch threatens to turn some of us lunatic, we wonder if we didn't really invent those winds. It might not even occur to us during those times that they might just as well have invented us by slinging before what we were a new force that we had to deal with. The genius loci of this place is primitive enough to receive our tumblings-about in the weather as signals crying for sanctuary, but also as signals which say, "Being buffeted about is our lot," for in winds mesquites rarely break. Their delicate, thin leaves mainly shimmer, just as we do when streaking past a threat great enough to change the sky's color, to give it a good stinging texture. Then we know who we are: creatures forever in process, whose hard, clayey hearts learn how to fly directly back into our bloodshot eyes. Then in our dreams we're back in spring, and as youthful and unformed as the year. The winds that blow all around us are also blowing within us.

Hurricane Alicia: The Second Night
Paul Ruffin

(Hurricane Alicia struck the Texas coast August 19, 1983.)

Going through my study someday, the kids will find among the mounds of papers and books and magazines, the hundreds of stacks of folders, the bookcases and file cabinets jammed to the brim— somewhere they will find a brown envelope labeled simply Alicia and inside it a crimped and crumpled manila file folder. When they open the folder they will find nothing inside, for the folder is the story.

The last thing we saw on television of Hurricane Alicia that day fifteen years ago, it was a tight green doughnut well south of Huntsville, spinning counter-clockwise and sprinkled with red and yellow glitter, like something a child would be drawn to at a bakery. Then the wind whipped up, lightning began, and the television fell to dark, along with the rest of the house.

For those who have lived through major hurricanes, this storm, now well inland and losing strength, would have been a mere nuisance. During the monstrous Camille, which devastated the Mississippi Coast in 1969, my wife (then a teenager) hunkered down with her family in Moss Point while the eye passed a scant thirty miles to the west. She had been through much worse than Alicia had to throw at us. But when she endured Camille, she was not seven months pregnant and the house it buffeted was not one she had spent years working on.

For hours we listened as the wind howled along the eaves and thunder vibrated the hill; we mopped up water driven under and around the windows and kept a vigilant eye on the great pine out front that leaned toward the room we had already prepared for the child to come. We watched and we waited and the storm trundled off to the north.

That evening, totally enervated by the tension and physical exertion of the day, we ignored the absence of electricity, went to bed early, and slept like the dead. The rain had cooled everything off, and a moderate wind blew all night. It was not a bad night for sleeping.

In the thick heat next morning we picked up debris around the place, going inside often to see whether the power was back. Noon passed—no electricity. Another call to Gulf States Utilities—no promises. Mid-afternoon I cleaned out the freezer and distributed the contents among friends whose power had been restored.

"Well, it may be dark before we get it back," I told her as we sat on the back porch in the twilight watching the lights burning in Jim Shaddock's kitchen behind us. We could hear his air conditioner purring away.

"I still don't understand how Joan and Jim have it and we don't. It's not much more than a hundred feet to their house."

I tried to explain the nature of the antiquated electrical grid we were on, but a hot, tired, seven-months-pregnant woman is not a good listener.

"We're not going to get electricity tonight, are we?" The last traces of sun had slipped out of the trees, and her voice had a faint, faraway hopelessness to it, like that of a wee, watery child drifting away from a lifeboat in the dark.

"Aw, cheer up. We're sure to get it tomorrow. We'll make do. It's no worse than those folks had it every night in August when this house was first built, no worse than we had it growing up, with nothing but Sears window fans."

"Oh, yes it is. In 1935 they didn't even know what an air conditioner was. Anything under 80 degrees was cool to them in summer. But we've been there: We've been cool like they never were in August. That's the difference—knowing what we're missing, knowing," she said with a pitiful sigh, "what Joan and Jim have right now."

She hoisted her baby-laden belly out of the chair she'd been sprawled in. "And besides, those people had FANS whose blades TURNED. Forget the air conditioner for a minute. We've got an attic fan and seven—count them: SEVEN—ceiling fans, and three oscillating fans, and not a single blade is turning! What I wouldn't give to hear that squeak, squeak, squeak of our old Sears window fan." She stormed off into the kitchen and rinsed her face at the faucet.

I finally coaxed her upstairs into a tub of cold water and cooled her down. Later, using a candle for light, we ate a bucket of fried chicken from KFC on the front porch. She was still in a foul mood. A woman well along in her pregnancy will tolerate very little from man and nature. She is not a figure of fun.

"I'm sweating like a hog again."

I laughed and pitched a chicken bone off into the azaleas for whatever creature might want it. "Hogs don't sweat."

"How do you know what hogs do or don't do? And don't throw chicken bones in the azaleas."

She was beginning to get really mean. I kept trying to recall something I'd read in the literature from Gypsy Perry's childbirth classes, something about "no matter how much they abuse you, remain calm and supportive."

"Well," I tried, "hogs don't sweat. They wallow in mud and the evaporation that follows cools them. That's just about all I know about hogs. I mean, besides their being good at breakfast."

"I don't know anything about them, but if what you say is true, they have more sense than people. I'm going to wallow in that cold water again." So we went upstairs and she got back into the tub.

While she was soaking, I pulled the mattress onto the floor and slid it beneath the one screened window in our bedroom where if any lost and lonesome breeze did happen by, it would fall in on us. When she came to bed she was cool enough to drop easily off to sleep, but I thought I'd better fan her for a while to make certain that she didn't get hot again and wake up. So I got a file folder and swished it back and forth her length and listened to the night. It was hot and close and not a breath of wind stirred the trees. I could hear the whine of trucks on the distant interstate, every rustle of leaves—cat, bird, dog, whatever—and every razz of the tree frogs and crickets. It was all strangely comforting, spooky, like I had finally found my reason for being.

After an hour or so I began to separate the creature noises into conversations:

"Come over," a male tree frog would say.

"Not now," came the answer.

"Why not?"

"Because."

"Sometime?" asked he.

"May-be," said she.

"Tonight?" asked he.

"No way," said she.

And then I would drift into another conversation. For hours it went on, for long hours.

Her voice came out of the dark: "I feel like I'm going to throw up."

I was nodding, almost in full sleep, and dreaming about a pair of tree frogs, so the first thing. I said was, "Tonight?"

"Right now," said she. And she rolled off the mattress. I rushed her to the bathroom, the best one can rush a ponderous pregnant woman in the dark, submerged her in cool water, and rinsed her until she subsided.

"Why couldn't this have happened in March or November?"

"Because there are no hurricanes those months."

"You might know. Nothing ever turns out right."

"Why don't you try to cheer up? Let's go back to bed and do some more Gulf States jokes."

"OK. I'll try."

Back on the mattress she said, "Let me see ... . All right. Knock, knock."

"Who's there?"

"GSU."

"GSU who?"

"GSU sure we'll ever get our lights back?" She tried to laugh. I tried to laugh, but the more I thought about the joke, the less I liked it.

"I'm sorry, Honey, but that just doesn't make any sense."

"Yes it does. Gee, is you sure we'll—"

"I know, I get that. But you've got the Gulf States man asking it."

"Well, you're dumb if you don't think that's funny," she snarled, "but I'm too hot and tired to care. I'm miserable, my freezer food's scattered all over the country, my kitchen is dead, the Shaddocks have power and we don't, and the baby's squirming. All I want is for tomorrow to come and that air conditioner to come back on. I want fan blades to turn!"

"Aw, relax," I tried to soothe her. We'll have something to tell our kids. We may not go two nights without electricity again the rest of our lives."

"And we may go a week before we get it back."

"In a few months we'll look on this as something really memorable. We'll laugh. We'll be glad it happened."

She didn't respond to that, so I started the file folder up again and kept at it until her breathing evened out and deepened. I fanned on in that dark, hot house, a man in strange harmony with his world, one with the frog-loud night and the sleeping, child-heavy woman beside him.

Hot

Some Balance Is at Stake

Chip Dameron

Quick nights give way to weeks of sun
in Texas, in August. Things take
their goings slow, or risk the stun

of unpent heat, whose blast can bake
the earth into a shattered pane.
So people turn to beer and lake

for respite; cranky kids complain.
It seems some balance is at stake—
grass yellows, life takes on its stain.

September's no better: days break
out of the dark dry as parched grain.
Then the skyline blackens; winds wake

the dust and drive the drops they've spun;
coolness descends on rock and snake;
dreams lengthen; October's begun.

La gente en junio
David Bowles

a dokugin hankasen

Barrios are teeming,
alive with raucous laughter—
summer has begun.

Sallow face at a window—
la vecina, phone in hand.

The raspa man comes
pushing his broken-down cart—
kids flock for snow cones.

Comadres in housecoats chat
beside the sidewalk, brooms poised.

And there's la güera,
walking to the store with an
entourage of boys.

Don Mario stands watching as
El Maistro stuccoes his house.

Doña Petra kneels
amidst her blue mistflowers,
crowned with butterflies.

In the placita, old men
play dominoes, reminisce.

The next street is blocked
to serve the loud World Cup dreams
of young soccer stars.

Smiling priests—one Mexican,
one Chinese—visit widows.

Alone in his room,
unbeknownst to anyone,
el Licenciado has died.

El Tuerto Guzmán slips weed
into a customer's hand.

Locked in for the day,
five-year-old Flora awaits
her working mother.

Amidst shady mesquites,
Sara reads fate in your palm.

Mr. Cruz, "el Sir,"
nurses the first hangover
of his break from kids.

Tangled in hand-me-down sheets,
newlyweds make hungry love.

Los Sánchez pile thick
into the family Bronco—
the ocean beckons

And the splendor of the sun
will illuminate the way.

Hot Summer Nights

Jean Jackson

Ice trays with ratchet handles
   kachunk, kachunk
Aluminum tumblers of lemonade
   rainbow-hued
   beaded with sweat
Windows opened wide
Moths beating wings
   against screens
Tick tick tick of overhead fan
Sunburned shoulders slathered
   with Noxzema
Shortie p.j.s
A pallet on the floor
   down where it's cool

One annoying mosquito
   buzzing in my ear

Humidity

Larry D. Thomas

(June in Houston, Texas)

is relative, but so high
his sweat, instead
of evaporating
and cooling his body,
deepens in little pools

and wobbles in droplets
fattening so they burst,
trickling down his chest
to his sopping shorts,
glazing his skin

with the gleaming coat
of a salty, liquid hell
whose phantom flames
burn him any way
but swiftly up,

fuzzying his thinking,
dragging out for hours
the feverish, dry-skinned,
rapid-pulsed delirium
of heatstroke.

Montrose in August

Marilyn Robitaille

She is white hot
Naked, alone
Skin against the sheets
Sweat pooling
Midnight in August
One single window
Open to the city
Montrose in Houston
   her territory
No air, only notes of jazz
Gathering like a storm
To soothe her
She dreams of slow rain
Then realizes her mistake
Texas summer is a demon
Dancing on her grave, laughing
She gathers herself
Sits on the side of her bed
   to think, head in hands
She is in hell, fires burning
Wishing for home, for Montana mountains
Wishing for cobalt blue and breezes
Wishing for a liquid lover to cool her down
He will not come
This is August in Montrose
Heat

Toes
Sally Clark

My toes are swollen
with the heat
like fat sausages
cooked to plump.

Last week they were
long and thin
like extra fingers
for gripping pencils.

One day, you're
the graceful doe
the next day,
you're pork.

And all because
the sun hung
around and heated
up the pan.

Heat Wave
Sarah Cortez

No one wants
      to go outside
            where even

this year's lizards
      are browned
            to a crisp, and

smallish. They
      skitter to shade
            across walks

before sun's torch
      can flame their
            evanescence.

Taking the Heat off the Valley
Jan Seale

Tell someone upstate you're from the Valley and they make a sound like they've just been hooked up to a respirator. "Oh, the Valley! It's so hot down there!" While you're wetting your lips for a mild remonstrance, they add by way of apology, "Of course, it's the humidity. How do you *stand* it?"

If they don't faint altogether from this one-sided free-associating, you try to get across a basic tenet: The Valley is not any hotter or any more humid than much of the rest of Texas. And a basic corollary: Living in the sub-tropics is not exactly exile on Elba.

The National Weather Service at Brownsville reports an average yearly high humidity of 76 percent. Compare this to Corpus Christi at 76 percent, Houston at 75 percent, and Dallas, Austin and San Antonio at 67 percent. It's only when you get to Amarillo, at 56 percent, or El Paso, at 41 percent, that you have to worry about flakey scalp.

Okay, okay, it's *somewhat* humid in the Valley. So shoes in the back of the closet get a little cradle cap, and mushrooms have been known to sprout indoors on carpets. We're not spending a minute bemoaning the fate of people who expect their wet bathing suits hanging on the line to be dry in the morning, or who leave the chips sack open all night and are surprised that they taste like oak leaves the next morning.

We never gave the heat or humidity a second thought until someone invented the dreaded Heat Index. Now, if the thermometer reading is 90 degrees and the humidity is 85 percent, we go around martyred, telling ourselves we're enduring 117 degree heat. Only when 90 degrees meets up with a relative humidity of 30 percent—probably some July day at noon three miles east of El Paso—is it *really* 90 degrees.

And how did the Valley draw a bum rap on heat-via-humidity? In my scientific search for the definitive answer, I asked a meteorologist forecaster in Brownsville. "I don't know," he said. "People are much better off here than in New Orleans or Memphis. I've had humidity condense on my ears when I stepped outdoors in New Orleans at night." So much for scientific documentation.

The rumor is that Washington has not and will not invent a heat index that includes wind. If they do, the Valley will be sitting pretty because a sea breeze at about 12 mph sweeps across us daily during the summer. (That's why the Deep South lost the Civil War—no breeze.)

The lush vegetation in the Valley could account for a little more moisture since green plants give off water. Some people think the irrigation canals contribute to the humid feeling in the air, but that's iffy. Elevation, or rather lack of it, could figure. The Lower Rio Grande Valley averages about 100 feet above sea level, give or take an anthill or Indian mound. So any wind blowing directionally from the south, west, or northwest will be a downhill wind to the Valley, and such a wind creates pressure and thus heats the air like a heat pump.

Personally I think the Valley's had bad press. Someone says, "Whooeee! That hot ole' Valley!" and it's repeated like a junior high game of Gossip. McAllen often takes the dubious honor of "hot spot in the nation" but that's more likely to be in the dead of winter. One Christmas eve, when McAllen was the hot spot in the nation at 92 degrees, we abandoned our carols and hot chocolate around the holiday tree, put on our swimsuits and headed for the pool.

Of course, if you're playing golf, you probably want one of the 227 sunshiny Valley days. You notice it is hot when you play 18 holes of golf on one of our 31 golf courses. And yes, there are vast gardens to be tended, swimming pool waters to be stirred, *pachangas* where the social mores of swilling beer and devouring fajitas under mesquite trees must be scrupulously observed. If you think about it, there's a principle here: these activities are *outdoors* and it's going to be warmer outdoors than *indoors*.

Maybe outsiders think the Valley is the Torrid Zone capital because it takes them so long to get here and when they do, they're in meltdown. Say they start out from San Antonio or Austin driving to the Valley for a convention or a wedding. They're wearing the clothes they wore to visit a castle in Germany: pussycat-bow polyester blouse and no-iron blend French-cuff shirt.

They drive a while and then they get scared. All they see is cactus and mesquite and hawks circling overhead, which they mistake for buzzards. The land is so flat they feel like they're driving in a trough. They look at the map and find they're only in Alice. Couple more hours oughta do it.

They arrive in McAllen about 3 p.m., when the sea breeze has pushed only as far as Weslaco. Folks are struggling up from under mesquites where they've been shooing fruit gnats and dozing off the pinch of opium from the Valley's famous "1015" onions they had for lunch. It's all too much. The visitors just *think* they're hot. Actually they're in metabolic meltdown from being over-dressed and over-travelled.

We have a margarita waiting for these poor folks who feel that, the state map appearing gravitational, they have fallen hopelessly into the posterior exit of some cruel giant. We help them out of their civvies and into muumuus and *guayaberas*, put them under a ceiling fan on a porch and tell them to move their lips slowly or not at all.

We tell them not to unpack their night creams and irons, because our lovely humidity naturally combats wrinkles of face and cloth. We tell them to quit fussing with their hair—let it blow. We call attention to how their emphysema and eczema have instantly improved.

The U.S. Weather Service tells us that if the temperature is 90 degrees and the humidity is 60 percent, we're in the Rapidly Decreasing Work Efficiency Range. And if the water in the air should rise on up to 90 percent, our government declares that "nearly everyone is uncomfortable" and we're hovering in the Danger Zone of Heat Prostration.

These statistics are worth heeding. They tell us Valleyites we'd better forget any Puritan work-ethic-type ideas (which mostly petered out in the Great Westward Push anyhow) and, with something cool to drink, go sit on the patio and watch the grackles.

In the charming book *Following the Drum* (Univ. of Nebraska, 1984) Teresa Griffin Vielé, an army wife living with her husband at Ft. Ringgold near Rio Grande City in the 1850s, observed that in the Valley "the climate was very salubrious, and cholera almost unheard of."

So if you're into cholera prevention, come on down. Just don't write back up north spreading silly rumors that it's hotter'n hell down in the Valley. It's not. It's salubrious. Healthy, too.

Cold

At the Dairy Queen After the Snowstorm
Alan Birkelbach

He was surprised to see the ghost of his father
sitting in a booth toward the back,
his hands cupped around a cup of coffee,
his overalls ethereally dingy.

His father motioned him over
from where he had been sitting with his friends,
the other mid-forties farmers
who had volunteered to pull people from the snow banks.

His father reached up, took him by the shoulder,
and whispered urgently and sadly,
"You are the cars you are rescuing.
I thought I had taught you to be the tractor."

Then his father was gone. He was left confused.
He drove home in a cloud, skidding on the ice.
He retraced every path in his house, looking for markers.
He crawled into bed with his wife, pulled himself to her breast.

Respects
Alan Birkelbach

That Winter, when ice fell like shot
for days, turning the roads to glass,
Grandpa died all of a sudden
in his sleep.
Grandma went a little crazy.
She dressed him in a shirt,
sat him up in bed, then called
around on the telephone,
inviting everybody over.
And we all came, sliding slowly,
bundled, full of dread.
Grandma made sure
we all visited one last time.
Standing there, staring big-eyed,
we never stopped shivering.
In the barn
the dog spent all night
barking at nothing.

February Lament
Ann Howells

Pear trees bloom with little exuberance.
Who can blame them? On again/off again
winter casts a pall; I am well and truly lost
a half mile south of *Road Work Ahead*.
Punxatawny Phil or Staten Island Chuck
spies his shadow, scurries back to his den,
endorses six more weeks. I watch it on CNN:
celebrity groundhog surrounded by top hats!
And if he nips the mayor's ear, so be it.
We need a southern groundhog—amicable,
gentlemanly, no scaredy-cat who hides
from his shadow. Big D Dan, Houston Hank
or Ft. Worth Freddie, would pop from a burrow
like bread from a toaster, warm to the core
and ready for jamming. Now, there's
a groundhog I can get behind.

Whisper in the Winter

karla k. morton

Whisper in the winter
when clouds hang low and gray,
for Mother Earth sleeps sweetly
in her icy negligee.

Disturb her not with shovels—
don't insist that she awake—
for even rain has hushed its touch
with each tranquilized snowflake.

When the last leaves fell
Earth breathed a sigh,
curled up, and closed her eyes,
and slid to peaceful slumber
while the wind sang lullabies.

Whisper in the winter
her night is cold and deep.

Whisper in the winter
women need their beauty sleep.

Snow Day
karla k. morton

School Is Closed Due to Inclement Weather

How lucky are we, trapped in this frigid snow globe;
an unexpected birthday of ice with white bows;

a gift of time, wrapped tight
like twilight's newspaper - rolled and white;
waiting somewhere on the lawn.

In Houston, Waiting for the Killing Freeze

Kathleen Cook

you'll be looking round the corner a good while.
The one that takes out the golden dew drop
and bougainvillea is out there somewhere, but
you'll have to do most of the ruthless pruning yourself.

Don't bother trying to align days and seasons, rhymes
and reasons. The crisp fall in September and snow in December
we learned from reading primers? As likely as that hit man
who might curb your over-abundant plant life.

Do this: keep silent, constant watch.

Count the so-few days between the loss of stalwart sweet gum's
last brilliant leaves in January and its swells with yellow green
leaf buds in February. If only you worked as hard.

Get on your hands and knees, spring and summer, to see
the wild strawberries and yellow straggler daisies. Try to achieve
as much as these, with so little encouragement.

Come August, when you might despair because of a closed home
and refrigerated air, venture forth to see yet another round
of crape-myrtle bloom, a city graced pink and lilac above green.
Give thanks.

Wait, as only you know how, for the first cool breeze,
but watch as you wait; the coral vine alight with bees,
the hummingbird dipping in, for a quick sweet sip.

Invite the stranger in.

Snowman

Larry D. Thomas

(Winter Storm "Goliath," far West Texas)

Even a witch would kill
for the frozen, hairy carrot
of his nose. He cradles heaven

with wide-open branches
brittle as good kindling.
His eyes and smile

are chunks of holocaust;
his scarf a cruel, scarlet joke
auguring the warmth of his demise.

Snow in the Chihuahuan Desert

M. Miranda Maloney

A fit of snow like a tantrum despite the sun's persistence
in December when the trees unveil remnants of summer's
escapades and love stories. For hours the desert is clothed
in winter's white, grasses wear its armor, what life remains
retreats to burrows beneath spiny mesquites, the clamor
of birds' songs cease and we are high like winds in spring,
crazy with want to touch, to lick, devour the sky's uncoiling
as if we are young again when mother, on her knees, kneaded
snow like flour, rolled the half inch layer for a snowman, its limbs
like my body, weak and bony penned by puberty's demands,
punctuated with month's blood, every cycle a different tearful story,
and I, all wound up like a wrung rag, or a wire coiling, prayed to die.
Now the girl is dead, my mother, frail, still kneads flour for the warm
tortillas she bakes for breakfast. December comes laden with want
for a snow storm, but it is only desire, for nothing, not nostalgia,
will resurrect those days engrossed in white.

Extremes
Nathan Brown

I stand, freezing my ass off,
in Fort Worth's train station
here on a March afternoon.

And it's been a good winter
for Texans who wanna believe
global warming is a hoax, but,

if it does turn out to be real,
was certainly brought on by
aliens—or the government

in cooperation with aliens
as some conspiracy to avoid
any political embarrassment.

Either way, it's cold and sleeting
like a box of thumbtacks spilling
out of a disorganized angel's desk.

Yet, I am not looking forward to
the white-hot flames and humidity
of a forthcoming August either.

I like weather in moderation.
Unlike my tequila. Which...
come to think of it... would

really warm me up about now.

Three Haiku
Mark Butler

papery leaves soar
pennants
candescent in flight

old windows frame
sweet autumn, winter—
the road south

low winter sun—
an unmade bed
casts a shadow

Under the snow, a secret world
Michelle Hartman

The city plants thousands of pansies each winter
flower beds at stoplights, crosswalks
in front of switch boxes.
Their tiny purple and blue faces
push bravely against
the snow, singing their April
promise to everyone
only to be ripped out
and replaced with daffodils and tulips
at spring's first sign. But not yet—
the thaw as luminous waves of wet
northern light plays sleight-of-hand
against grey sky
create and dissolve horizons.
Chieftains and Queens
conquer and dominate
fall, fodder to the next round.
Pansy to daffodil, queen to pawn.
Lithe spring has yet to speak
yet to bless
what winter has given me.

X-Mas
Robert Flynn

I knowed something was wrong. I could feel it in the air. I could tell by the way the cattle was acting. The sheep was acting funny too, but you can't tell nothing by sheep. Sheep are always seeing something that no one else sees. Show me a man who listens to sheep and I'll show you a man who spends all his time building fences.

Now, a horse is sensible, except when it comes to another horse, and Bob had his neck out and his ears up like the sheep did. I looked over where Cletis was riding Sweetpea, and him and Sweetpea looked like Bob. I always thought Cletis and Sweetpea looked a lot alike anyhow; both of them got that close-eyed, long-faced look like they was better than what they was doing. Cletis must be fifty, near as old as me, and he ain't never been nothing but a pick-up hand, working at four or five different ranches. He's a good one, the only one I ever use, and he could foreman if he wasn't always right.

Me and Cletis had been out since daylight checking the stock. Folks think it don't get cold in south Texas and it don't until everybody thinks it can't and then it does. A norther blows in and freezes everything. Sometimes it freezes into ice and when it don't the wind is so cold you can't tell the difference. Why, I've seen snow. It's usually gone by midday, but folks and animals suffer when they're not prepared for it. That's why me and Cletis was out. We was moving the stock out of the wind and feeding them so they didn't suffer none.

When we was done I was ready to load up the horses, get in the truck, and head for the bunkhouse. The heater in the truck hadn't worked in four years but it was out of the wind. But Cletis stood around like he was sniffing the air. "I got me a funny feeling," he said.

"What kind a funny feeling?" I asked him.

"If I knew that it wouldn't be funny would it? It'd just be a feeling. Like frozen ears is a feeling." Cletis wasn't born more than fifteen miles from where I was, but he was in the Army once and he thought that made him smarter than anybody. Shoot, all he learned in the Army was how to march. He told me so himself. "Cletis," I sometimes say to him, "since you was in the Army, march down to the corral and close the gate."

"Let's run by the hunters' doublewide," I said, but there wasn't nothing at the hunters' trailer, not even a hunter, 'cause it was

166

Christmas day and they was all home sitting by the fire watching football.

"You think we ought to check the first house?" Cletis asked. Cletis was in the Army and he thinks he knows more about duty than anybody. "Cletis," I sometimes say to him, "there's more to duty than killing rattlesnakes."

"I reckon we have to," I said. I don't know why he asked about the old house. It was way back in Whiskey Rock Canyon, and in the opposite direction where I wanted to be. It was the old first house on the ranch, a two-room bare-wall cabin with whatever shingles and floor the wind and rats hadn't gotten. It never had running water or electricity and the only heat was from the old fireplace, but sometimes during deer season on a rainy day hunters would duck into it for a couple of hours, which was about all a body could stand. And sometimes wets drifting through the country looking for a job used it to get out of the wind. They never bothered nothing, but Mr. Hasslocker didn't like them staying there. He was afraid they'd steal something or eat one of his cows. Shoot, I ain't never seen a wet that wouldn't put a banker to shame when it come to honest. But I was supposed to run them off. Them was my orders.

I pulled up in front of the first house. We couldn't see no smoke from the chimbley or nothing, but we both knowed somebody was in there; a house with somebody in it just don't feel like a house that's empty. Even a horse knows that. And, whoever it was, I was going to have to turn them out into the cold. And on Christmas day. I turned and looked at Cletis. "Your Spanish is better than mine," I said. Cletis grew up talking Tex/Mex like me but pretends he forgot how in the Army. "Tell them to vamoose."

"Tell them yourself, you're the foreman."

The only time Cletis remembers I'm boss is when there's something he don't want to do. So I got out of the truck and walked over to the door and shoved it open. There ain't never been no doorknob but the doorjamb is warped and friction keeps it closed. I stepped in and it took a minute for my eyes to adjust to the dimness and all I could see was a pile of rags in a corner. Them hunters is all coat-and-tie folks in the city, but when they come out here they wear the raggediest things they got and when they get tired of carrying them, they just drop them wherever they are.

Then I made out a girl, and a boy was standing in front of her kind of protecting her, and he was saying something to me that I didn't understand. "Cletis, get in here," I yelled.

"What's going on?" Cletis asked when he got inside. He palavered with the boy for a while and then he turned to me and said that the boy was apologizing for being there but they couldn't find no other place and the girl was having a baby.

"Baby?" Sure enough, there was a little old baby wrapped up in what was either a flannel shirt or the stuffing out of a sleeping bag. "What is it?"

"Boy."

"Don't that beat all that they'd walk out of Mexico with a baby on the way."

"They ain't from Mexico," Cletis said. "They're them kind of people that nobody wants and everybody keeps running off. Salvadories or something like that."

"Well, they come to the right place to get run off," I said. "There ain't no place for them here." Cletis acts tough because he was in the Army, but I knowed he wasn't going to throw no woman and baby out in the cold, and he wasn't going to say much if I didn't. He turned and walked out the door. "Where you going?" I asked him.

"I'm going to chop some wood, you dumb horse jockey. The baby's blue from the cold, and the mama's teeth are chattering."

I picked up a blackened can they had used for a pot and filled it with water from the spring behind the house. I give it to the girl and she give it to the boy who give it back to her. His hands were fairly clean so I knew he had found the spring. I filled the can a couple more times 'til they had their fill then I went out and picked up the chips and got a fire going and helped Cletis carry in wood and then we kneeled on the floor because it was too cold to sit and tried to thaw out. Cletis cut off the tail of his shirt, dipped it in the blackened can and the girl tried to clean the baby a little better.

"Look at them shoes," Cletis said. They weren't really shoes, they were them kind of sandals made out of rubber tires them folks wear.

"How far you reckon they come?" I said.

"A far piece," Cletis says. "But not as far as they got to go. There ain't no home for folks like them."

"What about the baby, ain't there no place for him?"

Cletis give me one of them Army looks that's supposed to mean he has seen something I ain't. I threw some more wood on the fire and got it to going where we could stand back a ways and let it warm up the room. I watched the mama and daddy in the firelight. They was scared, you could see that, but kind of brave too. I guess you'd have to be to come as far as they had.

It got warm enough that the mama unwrapped the baby a little and I could see him. Leastways, I could see his head. He wasn't much to look at. His eyes was squinched closed and his mouth was puckered like life needed a bit more seasoning to suit his taste. And his hands was knotted up with a fist full of nothing. I didn't look at him long. When it comes to babies, give me a pig ever time. Some folks like lambs but a newborn lamb looks spindly and all legs. A pig is handsome from the time it's born until it's near a year old. With humans it's the other way around. They're borned ugly and some of them never get pretty. "Hey, Clete, ain't much to look at is he?"

"He looks like a baby," Clete said, but he hadn't never seen a real baby before neither. Like me all he'd seen was foals and calves and lambs and things that already got hair on them.

Then the baby began sticking his tongue out and his face shriveled up and his fists started to shake and he kind a bleated. His mama shook him around and held him close and I got scared. "You think he's gonna die, Clete?" I hadn't never doctored nothing but animals except for that time a bull near stepped Cletis's ear off and I sewed it back on him. And he held a mirror and complained the whole time that the seam wasn't straight. His ear does pucker a little but he always wears a hat anyhow and the only time you can tell is when he gets a haircut.

"He made it this far didn't he?" Clete said, and I knowed he was thinking about all them miles them folks had brought that baby to be borned in this place. That kid shore had him some tough parents. You have to wonder if they didn't think there was something wrong, them coming all this far and still not finding no good place for a baby to be born.

"What do you reckon will happen to him? He ain't one of us and folks are always gonna be wishing he had stayed where he belonged and not come trying to take away what's rightfully ours."

"You can't never tell," Clete said. "When you're little like that, you can be anything."

"Here we are looking at this little baby that don't look like nothing appetizing; wouldn't it be something if he growed up to be somebody? Why, he might go back wherever he come from and be a leader of his country. And you wanted to run him off like he wasn't nothing better than a wet."

"I didn't want to run him off," Cletis said.

"You shore would have if Mr. Hasslocker told you to, you would. Why, you could a gone down in history books as a bad man."

"What about you?" Cletis said.

I got a good eye for horses and cows and I ain't often wrong about people, but it does seem hard to expect a man to cull kids. I bet there ain't one in ten could look at that kid and tell whether he was worth keeping or not. I reckon we was all thinking the same 'cause the mama and daddy was looking at each other like they wondered what they had got themselves into. Cletis was staring at the fire and snorting like a bull that's done sulled. I got up.

"Where you going?" Cletis asked.

"I'm going to take the horses back to the house, feed 'em and and put 'em in the shed. Then I'm going to see if I can rustle up some grub. I ain't et, and I bet these folks ain't neither."

"Bring something to heat it in and some rags. And don't tell nobody." I didn't even answer him. I ain't stupid.

Well, dang if Mr. Hasslocker didn't call when I was back at the house trying to get things together. Leave it to a man who lives in the city to worry himself on a cold night. Sometimes I think he worries more about the stock than I do. I told him we'd moved the cows out of the wind and fed them. The woolies was bunching up under cedars and other brush. He asked if everything else was okay. I ain't no hand at lying so I tried to haw around it and he kept on until I had to tell him there was a woman and a baby in the first house and they couldn't leave. I didn't say nothing about the daddy. I figured the less said about him, the better.

"They got no business with my property," he said. "Soon as she's able I want them out of that house." He don't take care of the house or nothing, and I bet he ain't seen it in ten years. Shoot, he ain't been on the ranch since spring shearing, but it's his house and he can do what he wants to with it. And if he don't want nobody in it, then there ain't going to be nobody in it. That's the law, I reckon.

I got together some pans that I didn't mind putting in the fire and a whole bunch of rags and can goods. And I took my blanket and the only clean sheet, and the bottle of wine me and Cletis was going to have with Christmas dinner.

When I got back to the first house, I filled the pans with water and set them near the fire to warm, and stuffed the spare rags into holes in the walls to lessen the draft. Cletis and the daddy had chopped some more wood and moved it into the house, enough to last all night. Cletis had been talking to the daddy some more and he said they hadn't had no fire because they didn't have no matches, and that the baby's name was Manuel, and they had been walking for more than a year.

When the water in a pan warmed the mama washed the baby some more and wrapped him up in my good blanket. She didn't want to rip up the sheet so I done it for her, and showed her she was supposed to use it for diapers. She thought I wanted the baby and she handed him to me but I ain't never changed no baby so I give him back.

After the mama and baby settled down for the night, I took the bean cans to the spring, rinsed them out and divided the wine into three cans because I didn't have but three cups in the bunkhouse, ever one of them give to me by an insurance company. Me and Cletis and the daddy drank our wine, and ever once in a while one of us would throw a log in the fire. We sat up all night. We didn't talk much because we was men and there wasn't a whole lot to say. This wasn't their place, never was and never would be. They might just as well turn around and go back where they come from for all the good they done.

I thought a lot that night about things I never had no cause to think of before. I thought about when I was a baby and my mama and daddy wondered what they had. I bet they never thought their son might grow up and be a foreman of a big ranch like this. Why, for all they knowed they could a been holding a criminal or a president, although I don't think I'd ever made a president. My daddy told me, "You can show or you can shovel," and he never had a lot of respect for folks that made a spectacle of themselves.

The next day three hunters showed up in Christmas-gift insulated coveralls and new insulated boots. They was excited because weathermen were forecasting snow and they wouldn't be stuck in the house with their kids that was already tired of their new toys. They talked about tracking down a wallhanger trophy buck in the snow but I bet none of them ever got 50 yards from their four-wheelers. And none of them had ever tracked anything that wasn't in high heels.

Mr. Hasslocker had told them about the baby in the first house and they had to see for themselves. They all three had flat, white-washed faces and smelled like toilet water. One was a banker, and one was a lawyer, and the other got rich buying and selling companies he didn't own. They warmed themselves by the fire and said what a fine looking baby it was, which was a lie, and how glad they was to see him, which was another.

They clowned around with the baby and made remarks about the mama and daddy and got to joking among themselves about how they ought to call the baby Nick since he was borned on Christmas day. How they ought to give him a present. They was just showing off, pleasuring themselves. The banker give him a dollar. "So he'll never be broke," he said. The lawyer give him a pocket can-opener, "so he'll never go hungry," and the other one give him a cigarette lighter with the name of an insurance company on it "so he can set the world on fire." They was real proud of themselves.

They looked at me and Cletis like we was too dumb to think of something funny to give him. We didn't say nothing and they got to looking at each other like it was time to do something manful, like go off in their heated four-wheel trucks and shoot them a trophy they could hang on the wall back in San Antonio. They always talked about wallhangers but what they usually shot was milksuckers. They usually asked me to gut the deer so they didn't get their hands dirty and give me the livers and kidneys as payment.

"How long you think they'll be here," the banker asked, believing they didn't understand a word he said or the way he looked at them.

"Not long," I told him. "Soon as the mother can travel." That seemed to satisfy them.

Me and Cletis went back to work busting bales and feeding cattle. Cletis said he wouldn't be back for a few days. He thought his daughter might be in Uvalde. Cletis' daughter was like the army, something he didn't talk about much but that was always lurking in his mind.

I heated a can of chili and crumbled up crackers in it and had supper. I looked around the bunkhouse for something else them Salvadores could use. Some powdered milk they could mix with water in one of them pans I give them. All the matches I had and another cigarette lighter that I found in the hunter's doublewide that might work. I put together the rest of my cans, and wrapped them in a blanket I could probably do without 'til spring. I could drive to town and get some more groceries, maybe even have a mess of huevos rancheros before coming back home.

During the night I was awakened by rattling on the tin roof. Sleet. There wasn't going to be no snow and nobody tracking anything. I imagined the sleet falling through holes in the roof of the first house and piling up in the corner.

I ate cold cereal for breakfast and took the blanket of things to the first house. I knew before I saw it that it was empty. It just felt empty. I checked inside just so I wouldn't have to argue with Cletis whether it was empty or not. They left the pots I brought them although I told them they could keep them. They took all the cans empty or not.

I didn't think the mother could walk far. I called a while but got no answer. I got in the truck and slowly drove around the pasture looking for them in the brush or out of the wind in a draw, honking until the cattle thought I was calling them to feeding and followed me. I stopped, drove them off and drove away fast until they got discouraged and gave up. I saddled Sweet Pea because she was good at climbing rocks and trailered her to a couple of brushy canyons I thought they might have pushed into to get out of the wind. I saw nothing except two of the hunters who had slept late thinking there would be tracks in the snow. The hunters hadn't seen anything either.

About dusk I rode Sweetpea up the two highest ridges looking for smoke or campfire. I was cautious riding up the second ridge until the moon came out, but Sweetpea was a good rock jumper. I saw nothing. Under the full moon the ride down wasn't as scary as I thought until we rode into the black shadow of the ridge. Sweetpea stumbled once and skidded on the rocks twice. She was shaking all over and I got off, stroked her back, scratched her ears and when I got back in the saddle she made it to the bottom without a problem. We was both glad to see the trailer.

I don't know what happened to them Salvadores. I reckon they're out there somewhere still looking for a place to light for a while.

Advent's End
Bryce Milligan

Fog clogs the highway but clears the mind of all but the tail
lights wavering in and out of focus as distance and density compete for
attention with the black ice creeping across the asphalt the further north
you get, transiting both map and memory as you recall another winter
drive toward another death bed fifty-six years ago, the night a cop
pulled your father over somewhere between Estilene and the bridge
over the dry-as-Ezekiel's-bones Prairie Dog Town Fork of the Red River
for speeding in a midnight blizzard, and it was only when you heard
your father explain that his father was dying that very night in a hospital
still a hundred miles away that your seven-year-old self understood that
all journeys can end without arriving at an appointed end—just a slide
and a thump, barely audible through the downy snow-thick air, just a
wheezing cough and a gasp, just a glance away from the business of
staying alive long enough to earn a wistful moment or two of longing or
regret or admiration in the tumbled memories of those left behind,
perhaps no more than an image, enshrined in the mind for no apparent
reason, like that other winter night when you were too old to believe in
Santa but were determined to believe simply because you did not want
to *not* believe when you snuggled beneath your grandmother's quilts
(three deep—oh, we were quilt-rich back then) when at the fringe of
sleep you saw your father in the swirling white cold beyond the rimed
and rattling panes bringing in the gift only Santa could bestow because
only Santa could know and the option of believing because you did not
want to not believe was abruptly null, your faith sucked into that void
from which faith in anything other than the present moment never
returns without its twin shadows of guilt and doubt, shadows that cloud
at once the meaning of yesterday and the potential of tomorrow as
thoroughly as the fog clogs this highway yet lenses all time into
momentary focus when you hear the dead calling you to breakfast from
the kitchen on Christmas morning and you smell the sage and pepper-
rich sausage your grandfather had slaughtered, butchered and smoked
only weeks before, and grandmother's biscuits and turkey hash and the
strawberry preserves made from your own labor the preceding spring
when the ruby fruits stained your hands as if . . . and here speculation
falters as memory stumbles, and you are parking your car in the hospice
parking lot because yes, if you refuse to die in a corporation hospital
they will be happy to rent you a room in which you can die at your

174

leisure, and you lean back, exhausted by hours of hyper concentration, minding the road, fighting the ice, entering the ghostly vortices that envelop the car as if to enshroud it but engine heat keeps the pall from forming on the hood although snow begins to freeze on the windshield almost at once, so you hesitate to shut off the ignition, reluctant to leave because to quit the car is to quit the dream and to step again into the storm.

Green

Indolence in South Texas

Steven P. Schneider

All afternoon on a warm December day
Three red-eared sliders

Hug the floating log on curlew pond,
Basking in the sunlight

After days
Of cold rain and fog.

Unwilling to budge,
Their necks outstretched,

They soak in as much sun
As the day will offer,

Much like Winter Texans
Reclining in lounge chairs

Outside their RV's,
Content to think of nothing at all.

Hawk-watch
Jim LaVilla-Havelin

sometime in a too warm February
two red shouldered hawks sat atop our
security light amused with watching
us on our back porch and our cats

flew to the first twiggings of what would
be a nest, and continued its construction
high in a live oak behind the house
visible from our kitchen window

all month, teetering back to cool and into March
we watched them, build and nest, swoop and
call, consider whether the Subaru beneath them
was a threat, decided, not

watched them into the time change,
into spring, through Palm Sunday and wild-
flowers, and always we looked, adjusting field glass
lenses, listening for smaller sounds

across what passes for seasons in South Texas,
each morning we'd look into the slow-greening
tree, slowly making it hard, harder for us to see—
red shouldered March sunlight shadow hawk

home   hope   watch.

A Little Flower
karla k. morton

> *'Just living is not enough,' said the Butterfly,*
> *'one must have sunshine, freedom, and a little flower.'*
>   Hans Christian Anderson

Sunbathing beneath the pear tree,
her lime green leaves flirting
in front of jealous oaks,
she called me outside;
the early warmth, an invitation
to shed my fleece and jeans and socks
down to a camisole and yellow panties;
white flowers falling on my skin
like scented spring snow.

I was told not to plant her—
her life, frail and fast;
but *she* is the brazen one—
the first bud, first blossom,
first plaything of the wind,
first desire of young bees;
laughing as winter beats his chest;
the girl with the longest summer;
her ruffling skirts of green.

March in Houston
Priscilla Frake

Spring adrenaline plumps the buds
with the purest form of energy: joy.
Every leaf reaches. Every petal
drinks. Every grackle struts like a peacock
in the caffeinated sun. Feel it course
through your legs, fingertips, solar plexus—
until you, too, gleam like a white rose,
like a heron tossing itself into wind.

Easter in Texas
Scott Wiggerman

There's little cool these mornings, July temps
in April all too common. High and dry,
this rainless spring, no moisture, no dew-damp
chrysanthemums or lawns. Some sigh and say
the wildflowers are the worst in years,
but what they mean is that there are no fields
of bonnets, no spectacle that allures
photographers like blue. The golden folds
on prickly pears have never shone so bright.
Despite the drought, the prairie's filled with spits
of red and yellow flair: Mexican hat,
Plains daisies, dogweed, Indian blankets.
They may be sparse and patchy, but no less
lovely—and without rain, miraculous.

Contributors

Michael Baldwin, MLS, MPA, is a novelist, poet, and creativity consultant residing in Benbrook, Texas. His book, *Scapes*, won the Eakin Poetry Book award, 2011. His poetry chapbook, *Counting Backward From Infinity*, won the Morris Memorial Chapbook award, 2012. He is also the author of a mystery-thriller novel, *Murder Music*, and a collection of science-fiction short stories, *Passing Strange*. Visit his website at *JMBaldwin.com*.

Alan Birkelbach, a native Texan, was the 2005 Poet Laureate of Texas. He grew up in rural, central Texas when the primary sources of entertainment were fishing, swimming, and the weather. Texas has always informed his work, all the way from wildflowers to the big sky to the pounding of hailstones. He is the winner of the 2015 Spur Award for Best Western Poem from the Western Writers of America. *Translating the Prairie*, an art and poetry book about the history of Plano, was a Prize Winner at the 2010 North Texas Book Festival.

David Bowles is a life-long resident of deep South Texas, where teaches at the University of Texas Rio Grande Valley. In 2014, the Texas Institute of Letters recognized his book *Flower, Song, Dance: Aztec and Mayan Poetry* with the Soeurette Diehl Fraser Award for Best Translation. Bowles is also author of the Pura Belpré Honor Book *The Smoking Mirror*. His work has appeared in *Translation Review, Metamorphoses, Rattle, Huizache, Asymptote, BorderSenses,* and *Apex*.

Nathan Brown is an author, songwriter, and award-winning poet from Wimberley, Texas. He holds a PhD in English and Journalism but mostly travels, performing readings and concerts. And he served as Poet Laureate of Oklahoma for 2013/14. Nathan has published twelve books. Most recent is *My Salvaged Heart: Story of a Cautious Courtship. Karma Crisis: New and Selected Poems,* was a finalist for the *2013 Paterson Poetry Prize* and the *Oklahoma Book Award*. His earlier book, *Two Tables Over*, won the *2009 Oklahoma Book Award*.

Mark Butler is a former journalist. He is a free-lance writer, editor, and more recently, a painting contractor. His poetry has appeared in *Red River Review, Three Line Poetry, Houseboat, Outward and Visible*

Signs, and other online journals. His nonfiction and news reporting has appeared in *The Philadelphia Inquirer* and *Forbes,* as well as business and trade journals nationally. He and his wife live outside Philadelphia, PA. They have two grown children and two grandchildren.

Native Texan Sally Clark lives in Fredericksburg, Texas. After retiring from the restaurant she owned with her husband in Fredericksburg, Sally decided to write poetry. She has been successful beyond anything she imagined. Her poems have won awards and been widely published, including the literary journals *Relief, Weavings, Chrysalis Reader, The Binnacle, Bacopa Literary Review* and five years issues of the *Texas Poetry Calendar.* Follow her at *sallyclark.info.*

Kathleen Cook, long-time resident of Houston, has enjoyed writing for all purposes since childhood. Teaching English only increased her enthusiasm for the charms of language. Topics seem limitless: tragic oil spills, violent bursts of spring, clamor of plants in the garden for her vote. She has been published in *Texas Poetry Calendar, Weight of Addition,* and *Untameable City, Poems on the Nature of Houston.*

Sarah Cortez, a Councilor of the Texas Institute of Letters and winner of the PEN Texas Literary Award in Poetry, writes for publications such as *Texas Monthly, Rattle, The Sun, Midwest Review, Southwestern American Literature,* etc. Her book *Cold Blue Steel* placed finalist in Writers' League of Texas Awards and PEN Southwest Book Awards. She co-edited *Our Lost Border: Essays on Life amid the Narco-Violence,* winning a Southwest Book Award and an ILBA. Cortez is a Texas Commission of the Arts Touring Artist.

Sherry Craven taught high school Spanish and college English. Her poetry collection *Standing at the Window* was published by Virtual Artists Collective. She has published short fiction, creative nonfiction, and poetry in numerous journals and anthologies and received the Conference of College Teachers of English Poetry Award. She is retired and lives in East Texas and is working on a poetry collection *Birds, Trees, God, and Love.*

Stan Crawford is an attorney and poet who lives in the Heights in Houston with his wife Dawn and their menagerie of pets. His poems have been published in *The Comstock Review, Poet Lore, Borderlands,*

Illya's Honey and elsewhere, and his recent poetry collection *Resisting Gravity* is from Lamar University Literary Press. Since 2002 he has been a board member of Mutabilis Press in Houston.

Carolyn Dahl moved from the swirling blizzards of Minnesota to the twirling hurricanes of Texas. Both a poet and an artist, (Grand Prize winner in the 2015 Public Poetry/MFAH ekphrastic poetry competition ARTlines2 and author of three art books), she finds intense beauty in weather's drama, but also feels compelled to document its destructive powers. Nature is often a topic that inspires her published writings (*Copper Nickel, Plainsongs, Camas, Hawaii Review, Colere* and 25 anthologies). More at *carolyndahlstudio.com.*

Chip Dameron's latest collection of poems, *Drinking from the River: New and Selected Poems, 1975-2015*, was published in 2015. Individual poems have recently appeared in *San Pedro River Review, Texas Poetry Calendar, Voices de la Luna, and Langdon Review.* A member of the Texas Institute of Letters, he lives and writes in Brownsville, Texas.

William Virgil Davis is an award-winning poet and critic. He is a past President of the Texas Institute of Letters and Professor Emeritus of English and Writer-in-Residence at Baylor University. His most recent book of poetry (his sixth) is *Dismantlements of Silence: Poems Selected and New* (Texas Review Press, 2015). His first book of poetry, *One Way to Reconstruct the Scene*, won the Yale Series of Younger Poets Prize. His poems have been published worldwide.

Ysabel de la Rosa is a fourth-generation Texan whose writing and photography have been published in numerous literary and trade publications. Her poem, "Each into One," was awarded first place in creative verse by Press Women of Texas in 2016. More on Ysabel at *YsabeldelaRosa.com.*

César L. De León resides in McAllen, Texas, and has lived along the Texas/Mexico border for over 30 years. His poetry has been included in several anthologies and journals. César is also an MFA candidate in Creative Writing with a Certificate in Mexican American Studies at The University of Texas-Rio Grande Valley.

Jeffrey DeLotto, Professor of English at Texas Wesleyan University, teaches writing and British literature, parents, cooks, writes, gardens and sails, in that order when possible. He has published in poetry, fiction and creative nonfiction, his latest book being *Voices Writ in Sand: Dramatic Monologues and Other Poems*, from Lamar University Press, and has a forthcoming historical novel, *Wings of a Just God*.

Having lived for extended periods in East Texas, Central Texas, and West Texas, Chris Ellery has experienced most kinds of weather in the state. Through hurricane and drought he has managed to publish three poetry collections, with a fourth (*Elder Tree*) forthcoming from Ink Brush Press. A member of the Texas Institute of Letters, Ellery teaches literature and creative writing at Angelo State University in beautiful San Angelo, "Oasis of West Texas."

Robert Flynn has spent much of his life and his writing reconciling the fundamentalist, jingoistic, Republican, Roosevelt-hating community he was born into (During World War Two) and his belief that redemptive violence is an American and a fundamentalist heresy. Violence may sometimes be necessary but to ride in, shoot the bad guy(s) and ride out is never redemptive. This is best illustrated in Flynn's *North to Yesterday*, *Wanderer Springs*, *The Last Klick*, *Tie-Fast Country*, *Echoes of Glory*, *Jade: Outlaw* and *Jade The Law*.

Priscilla Frake is the author of *Correspondence* (Mutabilis Press) and has also published poetry in dozens of journals including *Verse Daily*, *Nimrod*, *The Midwest Quarterly*, and *The New Welsh Review*. Although she has lived in places as diverse as New York, New Mexico, Scotland, and China, West Texas is the place she experienced the most culture shock. She currently lives near Houston, where she is a studio jeweler.

Laura Quinn Guidry grew up in New Orleans and has lived in Texas for 36 years, currently in Carmine. She serves on the board and coordinates literary events at the Round Top Family Library. Her poems appear in journals, including *Concho River Review*, *The Texas Review* and *Louisiana Literature* and in anthologies, including *In These Latitudes—Ten Contemporary Poets*. A poem is forthcoming in *The Southern Poetry Anthology Vol. VIII: Texas*.

Chera Hammons is a graduate of the MFA in Creative Writing program at Goddard College. Her work has appeared in *Beloit Poetry Journal, Borderlands, Rattle, Sugar House Review, THRUSH, Tupelo Quarterly, Valparaiso Poetry Review*, and elsewhere. Her chapbook *Amaranthine Hour* received the 2012 Jacar Press Chapbook Award, and a full-length book, *Recycled Explosions*, is available through Ink Brush Press. She is a member of the editorial board of poetry journal *One*. She lives in Amarillo, TX, and teaches at Clarendon College.

Jason Marc Harris lives in Bryan, Texas and teaches English at A&M University. He graduated with an MFA in fiction from Bowling Green State University and a Ph.D. in English Literature from the University of Washington. Books include *Folklore and the Fantastic in Nineteenth-Century British Fiction* and (with Birke Duncan) *Laugh Without Guilt*. Short story publications in *Arroyo Literary Review, Masque and Spectacle, Cheap Pop, Riding Light Review, Psychopomp Magazine*, and *Midwestern Gothic*.

Michelle Hartman's work was featured in the *Langdon Review of the Arts in Texas*, and is a native of Fort Worth. Her books, *Disenchanted and Disgruntled*, and *Irony and Irreverence* from Lamar University Press, are available from Amazon. She is the editor for the online journal, *Red River Review* and holds a BS in Political Science-Pre Law from Texas Wesleyan University.

Professional editor J. Todd Hawkins writes and lives in Texas. His poetry has recently appeared in *AGNI, The Louisville Review, Bayou Magazine, American Literary Review, Sakura Review*, and *Haibun Today*. He holds an MA in Technical Communication, loves Mississippi Delta blues, and in the evenings routinely loses to his wife at Mortal Kombat while the kids sleep.

Poet, scholar, translator, and editor, Kurt Heinzelman has lived in Texas for 38 years, entirely in Austin. Founder, Faculty Advisor, and Editor-at-Large of *Bat City Review*, he is a former Director of Creative Writing at the University of Texas, and his latest book of poetry is *Intimacies & Other Devices* (Pinyon Press, 2013).

Katherine Hoerth lives in Edinburg Texas, where the weather is a vast improvement from her native Wisconsin's ridiculous piles of snow. Her most recent poetry collection, *Goddess Wears Cowboy Boots* (Lamar University Literary Press, 2014) received the Helen C. Smith Prize from the Texas Institute of Letters. She teaches creative writing and literature at the University of Texas Rio Grande Valley and serves as poetry editor for Amarillo Bay.

James Hoggard, a poet, novelist, essayist, literary translator, and playwright, is the author of more than twenty-five books and the winner of numerous awards. He is now retired as the Perkins-Prothro Distinguished Professor of English from Midwestern State University. Twice president of the Texas institute of Letters, he is now a Fellow of the TIL.

Ann Howells has edited *Illya's Honey* for sixteen years, recently taking it digital *IllyasHoney.com* and alternating issues with a new co-editor. Her publications are: *Black Crow in Flight* (Main Street Rag, 2007), the *Rosebud Diaries* (Willet, 2012), *Under a Lone Star* (Village Books Press, 2016), *Letters for My Daughter* (Flutter Press, 2016), and *Cattlemen & Cadillacs*, an anthology of Dallas/Ft. Worth poets she edited (Dallas Poets Community Press, 2016). Her poems appear in many small press and university journals.

Charles Inge, a native Texan living with his wife, Dominique, on a bluff overlooking Lake Granbury, has the broad sky in its colors, seasons, and tempers laid out before him—muse and solace. His *Brazos View*, a collection of poems published in 2010, will be followed later this year by a new selection, including a few pieces about our Texas weather.

Jean Jackson, Michigander by birth, has lived with Texas weather for 51 years and for the last five has not complained about the heat. Through Northside I. S. D., she became a trainer for the New Jersey Writing Project in Texas and for the past 15 years has taught a writers' workshop at the Academy of Learning in Retirement (ALIR). Her poems have appeared in the *Texas Poetry Calendar*. She is past president of the San Antonio Writers' Guild.

William Jensen's short fiction has appeared in *North Dakota Quarterly*, *The Texas Review*, *New Plains Review*, and other various journals. His work has received several pushcart nominations. Currently, he is the editor of *Southwestern American Literature* and *Texas Books in Review*. Mr. Jensen lives in New Braunfels, Texas.

Vanessa Couto Johnson's forthcoming second chapbook, *speech rinse*, won Slope Editions' 2016 Chapbook Contest. Her third chapbook, *rotoscoping collage in Cork City*, is forthcoming from dancing girl press in fall 2016. Her first chapbook, *Life of Francis*, won Gambling the Aisle's 2014 Chapbook Contest. Her poems have appeared or are forthcoming in *FIELD*, *Blackbird*, *Cheat River Review*, *Cream City Review*, and elsewhere. She currently teaches at Texas State University, where she earned her MFA.

Southeast Texas native Laurie Kolp has much experience with hurricanes, most recently Rita and Ike. Author of the complete poetry collection *Upon the Blue Couch* (Winter Goose Publishing) and chapbook *Hello, It's Your Mother* (Finishing Line Press), Laurie strives to stir one's soul through words. Recent publications include *Yellow Chair Review*, *Pirene's Fountain*, *Leveler*, & more. Laurie is also a wife, mother of three, runner, teacher, & president of TGCW. Her website is *lauriekolp.com*.

Diane McMeans Kreger, "a Texan with an Oklahoma address," and her husband, Gary, live on their ranch in southeastern OK, with a small herd of cattle, several "free range" horses and chickens, and their beloved golden retriever, Emmi Rose. Diane, a graduate of Southwestern University, Georgetown, Texas, is a retired English teacher and Language Arts Coordinator. She now enjoys "life in the country," along with writing, reading, traveling, and working part-time as an English Educational Consultant.

Dave Kuhne is the author of a collection of stories, *The Road to Roma*, and a book of literary criticism, *African Settings in Contemporary American Novels*. He edited the anthology, *descant: Fifty Years*. Before his retirement, he was Associate Director of the Center for Writing at Texas Christian University and editor of *descant*, TCU's nationally recognized literary journal. Currently, he directs the Angelia River Press. Read a story from *The Road to Roma* on Dave's webpage: davekuhne.com.

Jim LaVilla-Havelin is the Coordinator of National Poetry Month in San Antonio and the Poetry Editor for the San Antonio Express News. Author of four previous volumes of poetry, LaVilla-Havelin's fifth, *WEST* will be published by Wings Press in 2017. LaVilla-Havelin teaches for Bihl Haus Arts and Gemini Ink in San Antonio. Retired after seventeen years at the Southwest School of Art as the Director of the Young Artists Programs, LaVilla-Havelin lives in Lytle, TX with his wife, the artist, Lucia LaVilla-Havelin.

M. Miranda Maloney is the founder of Mouthfeel Press, and the author of *The Lost Letters of Mileva* (Pandora Lobo Press 2014). Her work has appeared in or is forthcoming in the *Bellevue Literary Review, MiPOesias, The Más Tequila Review, Acentos Review, Huizache,* and other national and international journals. She is the Educational Outreach Coordinator for the Smithsonian Latino Virtual Museum, and editor for the *BorderSenses Literary & Arts Journal.* She lives with her three children and husband outside the Houston area.

Bryce Milligan was raised in Dallas, but spent a considerable amount of time in White Deer, Texas. He has lived in San Antonio since 1977. Milligan's work includes children's books, YA novels, plays, criticism and eight collections of poetry. He's edited several anthologies. He is the publisher/editor of Wings Press. His latest book is *Take to the Highway: Arabesques for Travelers* (West End Press, 2016). Milligan is the recipient of the TLA Lone Star Book Award, the Gemini Ink "Award for Literary Excellence," and St. Mary's University's "Art of Peace Award."

karla k. morton, 2010 Texas Poet Laureate, is a Councilor of the Texas Institute of Letters and Texas A&M graduate. Described as "one of the most adventurous voices in American poetry," she is a Betsy Colquitt Award Winner, twice an Indie National Book Award Winner, a North Texas Book Festival Award Winner, and author of ten collections. Her forthcoming title, *Accidental Origami: New and Selected Works* is due Summer 2016.

Octavio Quintanilla grew up in the Rio Grande Valley. He is the author of the poetry collection *If I Go Missing* (Slough Press, 2014). He is a Canto Mundo Fellow and holds a PhD from the University of North Texas. He is the South Texas regional editor for *Texas Books in*

Review and teaches Literature and Creative Writing in the M.A./M.F.A. program at Our Lady of the Lake University in San Antonio, Texas.

The poems, reviews and essays of Carol Coffee Reposa have appeared in *The Atlanta Review, The Evansville Review, Southwestern American Literature, The Texas Observer*, and other journals and anthologies. Author of four books of poetry and member of the TIL, she has received three Pushcart Prize nominations along with three Fulbright-Hays Fellowships and twice has made the short list for Texas Poet Laureate. She also won the San Antonio Public Library Arts & Letters Award in 2015.

Native Texan Clay Reynolds is Professor of Arts and Humanities and Director of Creative Writing at the University of Texas at Dallas. Widely published as scholar, book critic, novelist, essayist, and short-fiction writer, he has won numerous writing awards for his work, particularly for his novels, *Franklin's Crossing* and *Monuments* as well as a Spur Award for his story "The Deacon's Horse."

Sally Ridgway is a longtime Houstonian whose poetry has been published in anthologies, including *Big Land, Big Sky, Big Hair* and *Untameable City* in literary journals including *Gulf Coast, Texas Review,* and the newspaper *The Texas Observer.* She has taught creative writing through Writers in the Schools and The C.G. Jung Center and English at high schools in Galveston and Houston and at Houston Community College. She has an MFA in Writing from Vermont College.

Marilyn Robitaille teaches English and directs International Programs at Tarleton State University. She co-edits *The Langdon Review of the Arts in Texas* and co-hosts the annual *Langdon Review* Weekend in Granbury, Texas. Her work has appeared in *New Texas, English Journal, CCTE Studies,* and *Her Texas: An Anthology of Texas Women Writers.* Her film reviews are featured weekly in the *Stephenville Empire Tribune.* She also serves on the editorial staff of the *Journal of International Students.*

Paul Ruffin, 2009 Texas State Poet Laureate, was a Texas State University System Regents' Professor and Distinguished Professor of English at Sam Houston State University, where he was also Writer-in-

Residence. He was founder and Editor of *The Texas Review and Director of Texas Review Press. His stories and poems have appeared in many journals, magazines, anthologies, and university texts.* Ruffin's books include two novels, six collections of short stories, six books of nonfiction prose, and seven collections of poetry. He has also edited/co-edited fifteen other books.

Steven P. Schneider is professor of Creative Writing and Literatures and Cultural Studies at the University of Texas Rio Grande Valley. He is the author of several books of poetry, including two ekphrastic collaborations with his artist wife Reefka, *The Magic of Mariachi / La Magia del Mariachi* and *Borderlines: Drawing Border Lives / Fronteras: dibujando las vidas fronterizas.* His awards include a Fellowship from the Helene Wurlitzer Foundation.

Steven Schroeder is a poet and visual artist who spent many years moonlighting as a philosophy professor. He grew up on the High Plains in the Texas Panhandle, where he first learned to take nothing seriously. His most recent poetry collection is *the moon, not the finger, pointing,* published by Lamar University Literary Press in 2016. More at *stevenschroeder.org*

Robin Scofield, author of *And the Ass Saw the Angel* and *Sunflower Cantos* (Mouthfeel Press), *has poems appearing in The Malpais Review, Aster(ix),* and *Pilgrimage.* Her poems have also appeared in *The Paris Review, Theology Today,* and *The Texas Observer.* The next book, *Drive,* comes out in 2016. She is poetry editor of *BorderSenses* and writes with the Tumblewords Project in El Paso, where she lives with her husband and her Belgian Shepherd dog.

Jan Seale, a native Texan and the 2012 Texas Poet Laureate, lives in McAllen in the Lower Rio Grande Valley of Texas. Her poems are collected in nine volumes. Her prose writing has appeared in such places as *Texas Monthly, The Yale Review,* and *The San Francisco Chronicle.* Seale has held a Creative Writing Fellowship in poetry through the National Endowment for the Arts.

Joan Strauch Seifert holds an English degree and journalism/advertising minor from Texas University, Austin. Interests have included authoring a humor prose column in the *Southwesterner* weekly

Houston newspaper, writing advertising copy, associate poetry editor for *Voices de la Luna*, San Antonio literary magazine, and managing real estate home rentals. The muse's persistence has earned her places in a number of publications. Her poetry collection is *From Many Springs*.

Paula Noelke Starche grew up in a large Irish-German Catholic family on a ranch near San Angelo, during the life-defining drought of the 1950's. She went on to a career in medicine in Austin, where she lives with her husband, Nick. Her poetry and prose have appeared in the *Concho River Review, Louisiana Literature Journal, Rio Review,* and *Di-vêrsé-city*. She is the winner of the Texas Association of Creative Writing Teachers' nonfiction award in 2014.

Sandi Stromberg is a native Texan, but moved north as a child, then abroad, living in Switzerland, Spain, England, and the Netherlands. With a deep love of language, she learned Spanish, French, and Dutch, and launched a very successful freelance career as a magazine feature writer. She came to poetry late, after arriving in Houston, but has published in multiple journals and anthologies over the past ten years. She recently guest edited Mutabilis Press' new anthology, *Untameable City: Poems on the Nature of Houston*

Chuck Taylor, relocated to the Texas Hill Country between San Antonio and Austin, must watch the weather due to recent major floods, and keeps a canoe in his backyard. He's watched from his window small creeks turn to lakes. His loves to hang with his "It's complicated" family and artist friends. He takes photographs, does readings, publishes in a variety of literary genres, and performs magic for children's birthday parties.

Although Larry Thomas was born and raised in West Texas, he moved to Houston in 1967 and remained there until 2011 when he and his wife, Lisa, retired to Alpine in far West Texas. Far West Texas, especially the Terlingua/Big Bend area, has triggered a great deal of his poetry for the past several decades. A member of the Texas Institute of Letters and the 2008 Texas Poet Laureate, he has published several collections of poems, most recently *As If Light Actually Matters: New & Selected Poems* (Texas Review Press, 2015).

Sylvia Riojas Vaughn, daughter of a retired U. S. Navy SEAL, spent most of her girlhood on the Atlantic Seaboard. She's weathered blizzards, Nor'easters, and a hurricane. Her husband grew up in Kansas, and has ridden out tornadoes. A graduate of Southern Methodist University, she's worked as a professional journalist and as a certified English as a Second Language teacher. A resident of Plano, Texas, her poems appear in *Diálogo*, *Label Me Latina/o*, and *HOUSEBOAT*.

Lawrence Welsh has published nine books of poetry, including *Begging for Vultures: New and Selected Poems, 1994-2009* (University of New Mexico Press). Now in a second printing, this collection won the New Mexico-Arizona Book Award. It was also named a Notable Book by Southwest Books of the Year and a finalist for both the PEN Southwest Book Award and the Writers' League of Texas Book Award. Welsh's work has appeared in more than 200 publications.

Scott Wiggerman is the author of three books of poetry, *Leaf and Beak: Sonnets, Presence, and Vegetables and Other Relationships*; and the editor of several volumes, including *Wingbeats: Exercises & Practice in Poetry, Lifting the Sky: Southwestern Haiku &Haiga, and Bearing the Mask: Southwestern Persona Poems*. He is an editor for Dos Gatos Press of Albuquerque, New Mexico.

Steve Wilson's poems have appeared in anthologies and journals nationwide. His most recent poetry collection is *The Lost Seventh*. He teaches in the MFA program in poetry at Texas State University.

Patrick Allen Wright was born in Beaumont, Texas, and he graduated from Lamar University in 1984 with forty-five publications, ten awards, and Lamar's first creative Master's thesis of poems. In 2007 Patrick made a two-and-a-half year spiritual sojourn to South Korea to teach English and to learn more about Buddhism, visiting over thirty temples, most nestled into or atop mountains. Returning to Texas in late 2009, he now travels Texas and Louisiana.

Editors

Terry Dalrymple was born in Michigan but was transplanted to the Texas Hill Country at age three. Other than summer road trips to over half of the U.S. states, he has lived in Texas ever since. His current home is San Angelo, where he teaches literature and creative writing at Angelo State University. His hobbies are photography and landscaping. His most recent book is *Love Stories (Sort Of)*, published by Lamar University Literary Press.

Laurence Musgrove is a native Houstonian and graduated from Southwestern University in Georgetown, Texas. He has survived a flash flood on the North San Gabriel River and a Big Bend hailstorm. He is professor of English at Angelo State University in San Angelo, where he teaches creative writing, literature, and comic studies. His collection of poetry, *Local Bird*, is from Lamar University Literary Press.

www.ingramcontent.com/pod-product-compliance
Lightning Source LLC
Chambersburg PA
CBHW031955010726
47493CB00007B/2211